I AM HEALED

by Robin Smit

TWS | THE WRITER'S SOCIETY PUBLISHING

TWS Publishing
Lodi, CA 95240
www.thewriterssociety.online

To Dad and Mom, thank you for your unwavering support and encouragement. You have always reminded me that there isn't anything I can't do.

Most importantly, you taught me the value of seeking truth for myself rather than blindly trusting everything I read or hear.

I love you both!

Contents

Endorsement

It was an honor to endorse Robin's first book, "It Is Finished," an Amazon best-seller. That book was a great way for her to start a career as an author. Again, with great joy, I endorse her newest book, "I Am Healed." I don't usually make predictions. Nevertheless, I must predict that this book will be even a bigger hit than her first!

After reading the manuscript of Robin's new book, I would like to share a few highlights! Upfront, I must state that this book is not about typical healing techniques found traditionally in the Christian church, i.e., fasting and praying, binding and loosing the devil, denying the flesh, etc.

Robin states, *"I don't want to preach to you in this book what I believe about healing. I want to simply examine Scripture through the lens of FINISHED. I want us to put aside our preconceived ideas and beliefs on healing and our personal experiences in healing and just see what God says in His (written) word. And more importantly what He says IN and BY His Word (the Logos – Jesus)."*

The cross is the place of death where EVERYTHING died two thousand years ago. In Jesus Christ, ALL humanity sin, death, the law, sickness, disease, poverty, etc., died on the cross and was buried. And then ALL mankind rose together with Jesus in His resurrection.... leaving behind in the grave: sin, sickness, disease, death, poverty, etc. A brand NEW, never before seen humanity, FILLED with resurrection life, rose up from the grave IN Christ. And YET, a significant number of believers are still hoping for a someday manifestation of what He FINISHED.

Sickness and disease are not of biological origin. Its origin is in our false, distorted identity of not seeing ourselves as sons made in the image and likeness of Abba. Healing is an identity issue. You don't need to GET healed; you simply need to rise up in the revelation that you were healed two thousand years ago.

Some have asked the question: "Is God willing to heal?" I appreciate Robin's answer in the book!

"I love that the word we read as willing in our English Bibles is in Greek capitalized "Thelo." He wasn't just "willing" to heal; Jesus is "Willing." That's who He is. He is the Healer. He is Willing! I AM Willing to heal because Willing is who I AM!!"

She goes on to state: "So, I want to lay a foundation for our wholeness by looking at Jesus' final words, IT IS FINISHED. God's abundant life for us, this FINISHED life, is not to be continually healed but to know that we have been made whole. FINISHED! Completed two thousand years ago!

In John 19:30, Jesus said, "IT IS FINISHED" and then died, and ALL mankind and ALL that Adam had introduced into the world (sin and death) co-died with Him. The old man and everything that *hindered him from living an abundant life died with Jesus that day. The word FINISHED is tetelestai in Greek, meaning ended, fulfilled, accomplished, completed, and perfected. It means to bring to a close. It communicates the consummation of ALL things; everything is concluded. It is a perfect passive tense that denotes an action that is completed in the past, but its effects are regarded as continuing into the present without end.*

The work of man's redemption and salvation was completed, and the benefits of our redemption and salvation would continue in our lives! It was a full complete redemption and a full complete salvation (sozo – wholeness). Nothing was lacking in His FINISHED work. ALL was completed! FINISHED! Nothing else was needed or required from us. FINISHED indicates a position, a condition, a state of being, a RESTING place.

In my 25 plus years as a coach, counselor, and mentor, "sin consciousness" is perhaps the most damaging problem I have witnessed.

Hebrews 10:2 tells us that the worshippers, once purified, should have no more consciousness of sins. The consciousness of sins refers specifically to the belief in a present and persistent fallen condition of man that continues to potentially affect our status with God daily. It is the New Testament term equivalent with the tree of the knowledge of good and evil. And sin consciousness is our only tie to sickness and disease. BUT the good news of the gospel is that sickness and disease, sin and death, and ALL effects of the fall from God's perspective are null and void – defeated at the cross. FINISHED! But if that is not our perspective, then we will not see ourselves as dead to sin... dead to sickness and disease... dead to poverty... dead to fear... and dead to death! We will not understand that we are alive only to God. It is His life in us, and ALL the effects of sin and death are not part of our FINISHED life IN Christ.

The Father's perspective on the human condition under the New Covenant is Hebrews 8:12. It says, "For I will forgive their iniquities and will remember their sins no more." The Mirror Bible says "This knowledge of me will never again be based on sin-consciousness. My act of mercy, extended in Christ as the new Covenant, has removed every possible definition of sin from memory!" The word remember in Greek is mimnesko, meaning to call to mind, recall, and make mention! It is to mentally grasp it or to purposefully or actively remember. And it implies in its meaning to remember it with reward or punishment. In other words, Abba is saying, "I will not recall your sin, I will not mention it, and I will have no memory of the fall or its consequences." Abba didn't ever have a problem with sin conscious-ness...we did. He sees us ALL in Christ... holy, righteous, blameless, justified, sinless, complete, perfect, and WHOLE! And yet, religion talks about the fall as though it were an existing issue. Not under-standing that God is not forgiving sins and making people holy today because Jesus purged ALL our sins, completely sanctified us, and SAT DOWN!

God says we are clean, pure, guiltless, upright, innocent, unstained, sinless. This is who we ARE right now. We are whole and lacking nothing! But what we believe about IT IS FINISHED determines the quality and quantity of the FINISHED life we live out in this life. In Genesis 3:11, God said to Adam, "Who told you that you were naked?" In other words, who told you that you weren't whole, that you were lacking something? In truth, Adam and Eve weren't lacking anything. They were made in the image and likeness of God. But they believed the lie and consequently started living a life rooted in that lie. Having a false perception of themselves, God, and their world.

*The main point or finality of the revelation of our redemption is that **we ALL have a High Priest who SAT DOWN.** He is seated because everything that needed to be done is done. **He FINISHED ALL, He overcame ALL, and He sat down!** There is nothing left for you and me to do because we're co-seated with Him. There is nothing left for religion to accomplish. And there is nothing left for us to achieve. It's all perfected, completed, done! IT IS FINISHED!*

This quote lifted from the book may be the most significant insight in the book that you may not have ever considered.

> **"What did He finish? What was FINISHED from Jesus' and the Father's perspective?** He was telling us He completed or FINISHED Adam's original commission. He wasn't finishing the Father's works because Genesis 2 tells us that God had rested from ALL His works. And Hebrews 4 tells us that the Father's works have been FINISHED from the foundation of the world. So, Jesus didn't finish the Father's works. He FINISHED Adam's obedience. And now, from the Father's perspective, it is as if the fall never happened!" WOW!!!

> When He shouted *tetelestai* or IT IS FINISHED from the cross, it was a cry of victory! It was a declaration of the consummation of ALL things. He was saying, "The war or battle of mankind not knowing who they are and who God is, of struggling with sin and death has ended! It's done, it's over!"

His FINISHED work changed everything! He completely conquered sin and death. In Him, ALL of Adam died because of His FINISHED work. ALL the effects of death were canceled... sickness, disease, poverty, fear, depression, addiction, etc. His FINISHED work made the fall as if it never happened from the Father's perception. His FINISHED work rescued mankind from the dominion of darkness (from sin and death as a result of mistaken identity) and brought us (past tense! FINISHED!) into the kingdom of His Son. IN Him, we are whole, complete, perfect, holy, righteous, justified, healed, prosperous, etc. IN Him, we have peace with God. We are face to face with God (Father, Son, and Spirit) in an intimate, unbreakable, indivisible union with Them. IN Him, we are filled with ALL the fullness of the Godhead. IT IS DONE! ALL MADE NEW! IT IS FINISHED! And the result is that we are whole – nothing missing, nothing broken in our lives HERE and NOW.

In conclusion, this endorsement is only a brief "snapshot" of some of the biblical truths in this book that will be a great resource in whatever the path you may be traveling, i.e., housewife, minister, missionary, counselor, etc. Or just someone who wants to know "what is truth" concerning healing. This book just might be your answer.

DR. CECIL COCKERHAM
CO-FOUNDER OF GLOBAL GRACE SEMINARY

Introduction

"The great majority of the Christian world is still weeping at the foot of the cross. The consciousness of man is fixed on the Christ who died, not the Christ who lives. They are looking back to the Redeemer who was, not the Redeemer who is."

John G. Lake

The cross is the place of death. It is where *everything* died two thousand years ago. In Jesus Christ, all humanity, sin, death, the law, sickness, disease, poverty, etc., died on the cross and was buried. And then *all* mankind rose together with Jesus in His resurrection—leaving behind in the grave: sin, sickness, disease, death, poverty, etc. A brand new, never before seen humanity filled with resurrection life rose up from the grave in Christ. A humanity that was no longer bound by sin, sickness, disease, death, poverty etc. but a new creation who is immortal, incorruptible, sinless, deathless, whole, filled with divine health, complete, prosperous, etc.! A new creation who is as He is in this world and co-seated with Him at the Father's right hand.

And yet, a significant number of believers are still hanging out at the foot of the cross, or worse, carrying their own cross, hoping for a *someday* manifestation of what He has promised. But the good news of the gospel is that the cross changed everything and everyone!

> The message of the cross is the beautiful finality of it is finished!

> The message of the resurrection is the beautiful finality of the restoration of all things! The new creation—all humanity born again in Christ!

The abundant life we were created for was now restored... everything that we need for life and godliness is in us. We are partakers, or co-participants of the divine nature, living a life reflecting the realities of heaven here and now.

But if we cling to the cross, we continue to hold on to a *someday* way of thinking. Singing songs about clinging to the old rugged cross and exchanging it someday for a crown. Being *someday* minded! And thinking that eventually, we'll receive a crown and ultimately share His glory. But Hebrews 2:7 says, "He crowned us with glory and honor." This is not a *someday* verse. It is an aorist indicative verb tense: FINISHED! DONE! COMPLETED! We're not waiting for a future crowning of glory. We are carriers of His glory now, embodiments or physical expressions of His glory now.

Being *someday* minded keeps us from walking in the fullness of Him, in the fullness of the Christ-life in us. We are fully crowned. Crowned with His royal crown! Victorious in all things — victorious over sin, over death, and victorious over sickness and disease!

But rather than seeing ourselves as triumphant rulers and co-creators of our destinies because of who He is in us, we continue to cry out to Him for healing, deliverance, salvation, etc. We read the gospels and identify more with those who need healing than the One who is Whole and Complete and lives in us. Limiting our understanding of the healing ministry of Jesus to what we read in the four gospels will keep us in a *someday* mindset. And it will keep us looking to a sky god who might visit and heal us, rather than understanding that God dwells in us and His life is our life.

Visitation theology was the common understanding of the Old Covenant people. Angels stirred the water so they could be healed, prophets declared whether God might heal them, hands were laid on them, etc. But our new life in Christ is a habitation mindset, not a visitation way of thinking. He lives in us. It's His life that is ours.

We were not meant to need healing—healing was a FINISHED work at the cross.

But what happens when our understanding of New Covenant healing is limited to the four gospels? We will only see Him as continual Healer in the world. In other words, we will perceive sickness and disease as a normal part of life that He continually needs to heal. As something that we're stuck dealing with until we die and get to heaven someday.

And so, that kind of understanding of healing causes us to think that *if we can just touch the hem of His garment, or if He visits our healing services and passes by, taking notice of us and has mercy on us, then we will get our healing.* And so, we go to healing service after healing service, hoping we will finally get our miracle. Hoping that the minister will call out our specific sickness or disease and prophesy that God is healing us. We go time and time again to the altar and have hands laid on us for healing. Why?—because we have identified with someone needing to be healed of sickness and disease.

But that's not our identity. Our identity is found in Christ.

It's His life in us. We need to move past a "getting healed way of thinking" to the revelation that the will of God for us is divine health! His will is for our wholeness! Because our health and wholeness are FINISHED in us!

In John 5:6, Jesus asks the paralyzed man at the pool of Bethesda, "Do you want to be made whole?" This man had been paralyzed for 38 years. But paralysis wasn't this man's problem. It says that he had been in infirmity for 38 years. While infirmity does include physical sickness or disease, they are not the meaning of the word. The word in Greek is *asthenés* which means to be weak or without strength. It is the lack of strength or the inability to produce desired results, depriving one of enjoying life. This man was infirm; he was unable to produce the desired manifestation of health in his life.

> Rather than enjoying life, he was confined to his mat,
> watching life pass him by. Waiting on his "someday" miracle.

Waiting for an angel to stir the waters and hoping that someone would help him get into the water before anyone else so that he might be healed. He wasn't the only one. It says a great number of blind, lame, and paralyzed were all awaiting the moving of the water. What a difficult, hopeless situation—blind, lame, and paralyzed! The blind couldn't see if the waters were stirred, the lame would have difficulty being the first in the pool, and the paralyzed wouldn't be able to move at all.

All these people were infirm—they were unable to produce the desired result of living life abundantly.

They were lying by the Sheep Gate at the pool of *Bethesda*, which means House of Kindness. And Nehemiah 3:1 says that the Sheep Gate was built near the tower of *Hananel*, which means God's favor or graciousness. This pool had established a reputation as a place of healing. Tradition stated that an angel would occasionally come down and stir the waters in the pool and God's favor or graciousness would be available for the people. And the first one would get healed.

That's not the favor or grace of God in action!

Can you imagine the thoughts and questions racing through the people's minds as they waited to see if God would send an angel to stir the water? Would the waters be stirred today? Would God's kindness and favor be shown to them. Would He finally take notice and have mercy on them? Would they finally be healed?

Only one person would be healed when the waters were stirred: The first one in the pool—*the quickest one to respond.*

This man had been paralyzed for 38 years. It doesn't tell us how often he came to the pool seeking healing. Still, I don't think it's a stretch of the imagination to assume that it had probably been every day for most of his life. And because he couldn't walk and had no one to take him into the waters, he missed out on his miracle again and again. That would've produced disappointment, hopelessness, depression, etc. Or perhaps it caused him to just give up and sit there watching others get their healing and miracles. Giving up on the idea that he would ever experience God's kindness and favor. Thinking that God has not only forgotten him but doesn't see him! But then Jesus the Healer, or as Isaiah calls him the Master of Wholeness, walks through, and looking into his eyes with eyes of Love, asks him if he wants to be made whole. The man responded that there was no one to carry him into the water.

Jesus' question wasn't suggesting that there was something he needed to do or had failed to do to be healed. Our English translations do a poor job translating this verse. In Greek, the word 'well' or 'healed' is *hugies*, meaning sound, pure, whole, healthy, normal. It is to be whole and healthy. The word become is an aorist infinitive meaning it's not a progressive becoming but an already complete becoming—Done! FINISHED!

The Passion translation has in its notes: "Are you convinced that you are already made whole?"

Jesus was asking the man if he was ready to abandon how he had been seeing himself, and simply BE who he truly was, whole and healthy! Then He told him, "Rise, take up your bed and walk!" In other words, "Rise up, and live the life I created you to live! Enjoy your abundant life!" The word 'rise' means to awaken from sleep or death. This man, who had been afflicted for 38 years, looked into the eyes of the Master of Wholeness. And he saw his own reflection. He saw himself whole. And he immediately awakened from out of his infirmity—immediately awakening from out of his distorted sense of identity. Then he picked up his bed and enjoyed his abundant life!

I had difficulty deciding whether to title this book I AM HEALED, or I AM WHOLE. My dilemma was because this is not a book on healing but on the FINISHED work of healing and the reality that we are whole and complete.

This is not a how-to book with formulas or keys on how to get healed.

It is a book to empower you on who you are IN Christ... whole and complete in every area of your life, including being healed or whole in your physical body.

We read these accounts in the gospels, and we think Jesus is asking us today, "Do you want to be made whole?" We read into Jesus' words that He is asking if we have enough faith to be healed, or if we desire it enough, or for the right reasons. He's not asking us that. He's declaring to us—just like He declared to the man in John 5—are you convinced that you are already made whole?

Awaken and see yourself the way God sees you — WHOLE and COMPLETE! FULLY HEALED!

Jesus spoke to this man boldly! He didn't see him paralyzed, He saw him whole and healthy. He spoke the language of I AM to him. He spoke resurrection language! And the result was immediate. The man began to walk. All infirmity—the inability to produce results—was gone! He was now seeing himself as he truly was, whole and healthy!

In verse 14 of chapter 5, Jesus sees the same man in the temple and says to him, "See! You have become whole! Do not continue in your old, distorted mindset (*sin*); then nothing worse can happen to you! (Mirror Bible)."

Jesus is not telling him that if he sins, or continues in wrong behavior, he will be punished and become sick! NO! That was Old Covenant thinking! He's telling him that sickness is not biological in origin. It has its beginnings in the realm of our soul. Its origin is in our false, distorted identity; in not seeing ourselves as beloved sons made in the image and likeness of Abba. That's why having a book with keys to getting healed won't help you.

Healing is an identity issue. We don't need to get healed. We simply need to rise up in the revelation that we were healed two thousand years ago.

Prologue: The Glorious Creation and Redemption

All of heaven must have been at attention to witness this glorious event—the creation of man, the pinnacle of God's mindful design. Man was crowned with glory and honor as a lord in the earth, created in the image and likeness of God, with dominion over all the works of His hands.

Mankind wasn't created to be just a little bit like God; he was filled with the fullness of God. Abba knelt, face-to-face with Adam, imprinting this experience of intimacy in man forever. Mankind would never be satisfied with anything less. And Abba, He breathed into him the Breath of Lives. He infused Adam with all that the Triune God is: His love, light, life, goodness, mercy, and more.

God was merging His very being into Adam, pouring Himself completely into him, filling him with the totality of His life, Spirit, and faith. He injected His very DNA into him. The fall didn't change any of that. Mankind simply forgot who they were as sons made in the image and likeness of Abba. They spent almost four thousand years living in a false, distorted identity of their own making, seeing them-selves, God, and their world through a warped lens.

But then, the fullness of time had come! Eternity entered time. God came to earth as a Man to redeem His sons. As the Last Adam, He not only restored us to what Adam and Eve had lost but elevated us to what He, the Last Adam, is: sinless, glorified, incorruptible, immortal, seated on the throne.

Part One

The Eternal Foundations Of Healed

Chapter 1

We Need a Revelation of Wholeness

"Arise (from the depression and prostration in which circumstances have kept you) — rise to a new life)! Shine (be radiant with the glory of the Lord), for your light has come, and the glory of the Lord has risen upon you!"

Isaiah 60:1 (Amplified Version)

Isaiah is talking about a resurrected, glorified, fully redeemed new creation in Christ — the New Jerusalem, the Bride of Christ! And in Christ, we have risen above circumstances, and we radiate with the glory of the Lord!

In chapter 60, Isaiah says that we are majestic, a source of joy for every generation, wealth and abundance is ours, and we know Him intimately. No violence, no ruin, and no destruction within our borders. Our days of sadness are over and we permanently possess the Promised Land. He says that we are the glorious temple of God, adorned with even more glory than we comprehend! And, in verse 17, he says that peace governs our lives. The word 'peace' is *shalom*, which means wholeness and completeness. The Septuagint uses the word *arche* for governing, which means commander, prince, ruler.

Wholeness and completeness—FINISHED—governs our lives! Leading and overseeing every area of our life!

This is the abundant life He gave to us two thousand years ago. But most people are living far below the life described in Isaiah 60. Instead of wholeness and completeness overseeing our lives, we often think that we are powerless to our circumstances. And so, we continue to live life weighed down by sickness, disease, poverty, fear, etc. Why is that? It can't be because of an inferior redemption. Jesus completely 100% succeeded in His mission. So, the problem must be with us, in our understanding of who we are IN Him. Because from His side, ALL is FINISHED, and everything we need to live this abundant NEW life is already in us.

Peter said it like this, "He has given us ALL things that pertain to life and godliness."

All things are in us now, not someday, but *now*. Everything we could ever need for our physical life and spiritual life is already in us. Things like righteousness, wisdom, faith, divine health, wholeness,

prosperity, etc., all are already in us. So, why aren't we seeing a manifestation of these things? I believe it's because we're still striving after
them. Either by pleading with God to give them to us or trying to
manifest them in our own strength through our own faith.

For example, we've made healing about our faith rather than His.
And then, when someone's healing didn't manifest, they were told
that they just didn't have enough faith. But the truth is faith isn't the
problem! Because no one has more faith than anyone else. We've all
been given *the measure* of faith. The faith we have is His faith in us,
just as it is His peace, grace, love, wisdom, power, righteousness, etc.
in us.

His faith is already in us, and it is a full, complete, and perfect faith!

Paul said in Galatians 2:20 that our new life in Christ is living life *in
and by* His faith, not our own! We all have His complete, perfect faith
in us, but we learn to live *in and by* that faith at different paces.

Prosperity and health are part of His grace, and the good news of the
gospel is that we are to be prosperous and healthy in this life because
they are FINISHED works in us. 3 John 1:2 says, *"Beloved I pray that
you prosper in all things and be in health as your soul prospers."* The
word 'prosper' means to succeed, and it carries the idea of thriving
and succeeding in whatever we do. And the word 'health' is to be
healthy, in sound working order, and everything working the way it's
supposed to. It is to be whole! We were created to be successful,
whole, and complete in all that we do. John says that our physical

health, wholeness, and success in every area of our life are just as, or
directly proportional to, our soul prospering.

Coming from a Word of Faith background, I was taught that my
body's wellness and prosperity were measured by the degree that my
soul was prospering. In other words, to the degree that I was growing
in the word, to the degree I was renewing my mind, etc. *then* my body
would experience health, and my finances would prosper. But that
kind of thinking kept me from seeing my health and prosperity as a
FINISHED work solely dependent upon what Jesus did, not what
I do.

*John is telling us that we are fully redeemed in our physical
bodies, soul (in our mind, will, and emotions), finances, and
relationships in life—**therefore**, we should be experiencing
wholeness in every area of our lives.*

John wrote this letter to Gaius. He begins by acknowledging that
Gaius is walking in the truth, living out the gospel's truth with his
fellow men. And then he encourages him to live out the truth of the
gospel in his physical body and prosperity as well. The name Gaius is
from the word *gaios* and means lord. Mankind was created to be lords
of the earth with authority over all the works of God's hands.

We were created to succeed in all areas of life. Not someday
in a millennial kingdom... but right now in this lifetime, here
on this earth.

Healing and prosperity are probably the two most controversial benefits of grace in the body of Christ. Why are they controversial? Because most people have lived their lives experiencing sickness, disease, and/or financial lack. And it has become a normal way of life for them. And these experiences become their filter for understanding God... or rather *misunderstanding* Him.

When I teach about living a FINISHED life, most people want to know how to experience health and prosperity because they aren't seeing the manifestation of those things in their lives.

Many live powerless to things like sickness and disease because they don't know that God's desire for them is always divine health and wholeness. Believing divine health and wholeness is a "someday" event—after they die and go to heaven and experience a fully redeemed body. Believing that for now our body is subject to sickness and disease here in this life. But Romans 5:16 says, "We've been given an abundance of grace and the gift of righteousness, and we reign in this life!" I want the fullness of His abundance of grace and righteousness operating in my life continually so that I will experience reigning in life! How about you?

What we need is a revelation of wholeness!

Two words reveal our wholeness: salvation and peace. But unfortunately, we've watered down the meanings of these words. We've understood salvation to be just the forgiveness of sins and obtaining eternal life (making it about getting to heaven and missing hell). And peace has been downgraded to merely a feeling; a calm, the absence of fear, chaos, and anxiety. And so, we've missed the full meaning of these words.

'Salvation' in Greek is *sozo* and means saved, healed, delivered, rescued, prospered.

It is a word of complete victory, of being whole in every area of our lives: physically, spiritually, mentally, financially, and socially. Salvation is the answer to everything we need. It is to be undamaged and unbroken. It is to be whole and complete.

Our healing and restored health are benefits of our salvation. And financial prosperity and having a complete, ever-victorious life are also benefits of our salvation. He always leads us in triumph! Salvation and its benefits are not something we have to strive after. We already have salvation! It's a FINISHED work of Christ.

'Peace' in Greek is *eirene* and means to join or bind together that which has been separated.

It is the picture of a dovetail joint in carpentry because of its resistance to being pulled apart. It is considered one of the strongest and most beautiful joints. It is to be joined together into a whole. Paul said we have peace with God. The word 'with' is *pros* and means face-to-face. Peace with God is our unbreakable, irreversible, intimate, face-to-face union with God. We are ONE with Him. In Hebrew, the word for 'peace' is *shalom*, meaning completeness, soundness, welfare, peace, and wholeness. The Septuagint uses the Greek word *eirene* to translate *shalom* in the Old Testament verses.

Our union with God and our wholeness is the same thing. Our oneness with God means we are whole.

We have peace with God! We are entirely, in every way, completely joined to Him; and joined to all that He is! There is no separation. We are one with Him, in Him! Whatever is true of Him is equally true of us because we are fused together with Him as one!

In Luke 5 is the story of Jesus healing a leper by stretching out His hand and touching him. The word 'touch' is *haptomai*, meaning a touch that alters, changes, or modifies someone. The touch of Jesus transformed the leper's physical body healing him completely.

But He didn't just touch us; WE ARE JOINED TO HIM.
We are one with Him, IN Him. His presence in us altered,
changed, and modified our entire being.

We are irreversibly perfectly and completely joined to Him who is
Whole. Therefore, we are whole! Our wholeness is a FINISHED
work that happened two thousand years ago. It is irreversible and
indivisible. Our entire being (spirit, soul, and body) is forever altered.
Whatever is true of Him is equally true of us now.

> Romans 5:1 (NKJV) says, *"Therefore, being justified*
> *by faith, we have peace with God through our*
> *Lord Jesus Christ."*

> The Mirror Bible says it like this, *"The conclusion is*
> *clear: our blameless innocence has absolutely*
> *nothing to do with something we did to qualify*
> *ourselves; it is what happened to us, solely because*
> *of our Lord Jesus Christ's doing. Faith, and not*
> *reward, is the only valid basis for righteousness!*
> *Let us now fully engage this seamless union in*
> *our face-to-face friendship with God!"*

I love that! *Let us now fully engage in this seamless union in our face-*
to-face friendship with God. We are face-to-face with Father, Son, and
Spirit. We can't get any closer to Them than we already are. And
They are face-to-face with us. We are one with Them in Christ! Paul
said that we have been justified by faith. The word 'justified' is past

tense, FINISHED tense. It's in a passive voice, meaning that it happened to us without our consent, without our help, and it can't ever be undone or done again. And therefore we have peace with God. Nothing is hindering our intimate relationship with God. We are free to enjoy His presence, free to enjoy talking with Him, loving Him, and living life in union with Him. And as we do, we look into His face and see our wholeness mirrored in Him!

We see that as He is, so are we in this world: whole, unbroken, undamaged, lacking nothing!

We see that we are already healed, prosperous, and victorious in all areas of life!

Paul said we have this justification and peace with God through our Lord Jesus Christ. The word 'through' in Greek is *dia*, meaning completely, successfully through Jesus Christ. FINISHED! He alone is the Source of our wholeness, the Source of our peace! The writer of Hebrews said He is the Captain or Prince Leader of our salvation (*sozo*). Isaiah said He is the Prince of our peace (*shalom*).

I like the Voice translation of Isaiah 9:6. It says, "He is the Master of our wholeness!"

Ephesians 6:15 calls the gospel *the gospel of peace*. In other words, it is the gospel of wholeness! We don't need a revelation in healing or prosperity. Those are simply the benefits of this gospel of wholeness. We only need a revelation of the good news of our wholeness as a FINISHED work! Because with a revelation of wholeness, we won't be moved by circumstances that seemingly contradict it.

Instead, we will know that our wholeness is a FINISHED work and governs and rules every part of our life. And as a result of we will reign in life!

Chapter 2

Ephesians One — Chosen IN Christ!

He associated us in Christ before ₁the fall of the world. Jesus is God's mind made up about us. He always knew in his love that he would present us again face-to-face before him in blameless innocence.

Ephesians 1:4 (Mirror Bible)

Jesus did everything that needed to be done for everyone to experience wholeness, health, peace, freedom, and prosperity in every area of life. Just because we're not experiencing it doesn't make it any less true. Ephesians 1 is such a great chapter regarding our wholeness in Christ. The entire book is amazing, but we'll focus on chapter one because it contains essential foundational truths about our identity in Christ that we need to grasp to better understand our wholeness.

One New Testament scholar calls Ephesians "the high road of New Testament revelation." Another describes it as "the most excellent and majestic expression of the gospel." A.T. Pearson referred to Ephesians as "Paul's third-heaven epistle." C. H. Dodd hailed it as "the crown of Paulinism." In his book *Exposition of Ephesians*, William Hendriksen says, "Ephesians has been called 'the divinest composition of man,' 'the distilled essence of the Christian religion,' 'the most authoritative and most consummate compendium of the Christian faith,' and 'full to the brim with thoughts and doctrines sublime and momentous.'"

Ephesians was most likely written as a circular letter to the church in Ephesus, intended to be passed around to several younger churches in the region. Paul wrote it to encourage the Ephesian church and Christians to continue to walk in their identity in Christ. Scholars do not consider it a teaching letter, as Ephesus was one of the most well-taught churches. Paul spent more time teaching there than anywhere else, and when he left, Timothy stayed on to continue the teaching. This epistle draws our attention to the glory of God and who we are in Christ.

Paul talks a lot about the *ekklesia* in Ephesians. But *ekklesia* doesn't mean church in the sense of a building that we go to weekly to worship or a group of people who have prayed the "sinner's prayer." It is from two words, *ek* and *kaleo*. The word *ek* speaks of source, origin, and means out of. And *klesia* comes from *kaleo*, meaning to identify by name, to surname.

The *ekklesia* is the expression of God's image and likeness redeemed in human life. It is the body of Christ as redeemed humanity, the expression of God on earth, reflecting His image and likeness. The book of Ephesians is about our identity in Christ and the glory of God. The Greek word for glory, *doxa*, stems from *dokeo*, meaning the personal opinion that determines value. Thus, glory represents the view and opinion of God, as well as His nature and acts in manifestation. In other words, Ephesians is all about God's good opinion of you, who He says you are, the value He places on you, and His nature and life expressed in and through you.

Ephesians 1:1-2 says, *"Paul, an apostle of Jesus Christ by the will of God, to the saints who are in Ephesus, and faithful in Christ Jesus: ² Grace to you and peace from God our Father and the Lord Jesus Christ."*

Paul addresses this letter to the saints who are in Ephesus and the faithful in Christ Jesus. The word 'saint' is *hagios* in Greek, meaning holy or sanctified. While he is addressing this letter specifically to the Ephesians, all humanity is *hagios*. All humanity is holy and sanctified. Holiness and sanctification are not progressive, despite what you may have been told. That belief has kept people bound, thinking they are never enough and must strive to become holy or sanctified through their actions. But the truth is that we cannot become any more holy than we already are. We can, however, become more aware of it.

We are right now completely holy because we are as holy as
He is! We are not becoming progressively more holy in life.

It's not blasphemous to say we are as holy as God is! It is actually
agreeing with Him and affirming what He says is true about us. We
are made in His image and likeness—we have His nature. And since
God's nature is holy, we are holy. This is not about behavior; it's
about identity. His identity is our identity.

Colossians 1:21-22 says, *"Once you were alienated*
from God and were hostile in your minds because
of evil deeds. But now He has reconciled you in
the body of His (Jesus') flesh through death to
present you holy, unblemished, and blameless."

He said those He reconciled are holy. They are set apart from sin and
death and separated unto God. Those He reconciled are unblemished—without fault, without spot, without blame! And those He
reconciled are blameless—unreproveable, not called to account for
anything, unaccused!

Who has He reconciled? Who are the ones that are holy,
unblemished, and blameless?

In 2 Corinthians 5:19, we are told that God was in Christ (on the cross), reconciling *the world* to Himself, not imputing their sins against them. He reconciled the world. Who is the world? All humanity! In other words, everyone (the world) is holy, unblemished, blameless! This is who I am, who you are, and who all mankind is —*regardless of behavior!* That's the good news of the gospel! It is the good news that causes joy!

Our holiness is a FINISHED work.

Ephesians 1 is also addressed to the faithful, or we could say to those full of faith. But full of whose faith? The Bible says there is only one faith—His faith (Ephesians 4:5).

However, when we see the word "faithful," we typically think of it as something we do. But being faithful is not about getting a pat on the back for staying true to Jesus or being loyal and unwavering in our Christian walk. No, it is about being full of His faith. And we are all full of His faith because His faith is in us. We may not be fully awakened to all that His faith believes yet, but nevertheless, His full faith is in us.

Also, 'holy' and 'faithful' in these verses are not verbs. Paul isn't referring to those who act holy and believe in Jesus; they are adjectives describing those in Christ—holy and faithful ones in Christ. Holy and faithful is not what we do—it is who we are in Christ!

While I do think that believing is important, we've made it way more complicated than it was meant to be. We've turned it into something we "do to receive" rather than simply responding to what is true. Receiving is comprehending, grasping, and identifying with what God says is already true about us. Believing is being fully persuaded by His faith and identifying with what He says is true about us and what is already ours. Because as He is, so are we in this world. He is faithful, and so we are faithful!

We are to rest in His faithfulness because the bottom line is the FINISHED work has never been about our faithfulness; it was always about His! Romans 3:3 says, "What if some were unfaithful? Will their unfaithfulness nullify God's faithfulness?" In verse 4, Paul says, "Certainly not!" In 2 Timothy 2:13, Paul says that *"If we are faithless, He remains faithful, for He cannot deny Himself."* It's His faith and His faithfulness that we rest in—in every area of our life, including our health and healing!

Ephesians 1:3-6 says, *"Blessed be the God and Father of our Lord Jesus Christ, who has blessed us with every spiritual blessing in the heavenly places in Christ, ⁴ just as He chose us in Him before the foundation of the world, that we should be holy and without blame before Him in love, ⁵ having predestined us to adoption as sons by Jesus Christ to Himself, according to the good pleasure of His will, ⁶ to the praise of the glory of His grace, by which He made us accepted in the Beloved."*

Verses 3–14 are actually one long run-on sentence in Greek. In other words, it is one expressed thought. But to grasp what Paul is saying, let's break it up into sections, starting with verses 3–6. These verses reveal a purpose and plan older than time, showcasing our original design from before time began. In verse 3, it says, "Blessed be the God and Father of our Lord Jesus Christ, who has blessed us with every spiritual blessing in the heavenly places IN Christ."

I like the Mirror translation, "Let's celebrate God! He lavished every blessing heaven has upon us in Christ!"

The term "in Christ" is the cornerstone and foundation of Paul's teachings. It appears an estimated 160 times in the New Testament—and 36 times in Ephesians alone. It refers to what Christ finished for us, and as us. Paul tells us that every spiritual blessing in heaven is available to us right now in Christ. It's not something we're waiting for or hoping for someday—it's all available in us now. It's in the heavenly places in Christ. The translators added the word "places," and other translations added "realms" or "worlds." While these are not bad translations, they can cause you to think of a place outside of yourself or somewhere out there in a place called heaven.

And typically, thinking of a place called heaven causes us to believe that this is a someday verse. As in, someday after I die and go to heaven, then I will have every spiritual blessing. Or someday, as in when and if God decides to pour them down on me here, then I can have them. Connecting the "when and if" in our thinking to whether we've obeyed completely, been faithful, believed enough, etc. But in Greek, it just reads, "in the heavenlies in Christ."

The tabernacle was a type and shadow of heavenly things. Hebrews 8:5 (Berean Study Bible) says, "The place where they serve is a copy and shadow of what is in heaven. This is why Moses was warned when he was about to build the tabernacle: 'See to it that you make everything according to the pattern shown you on the mountain.'" The most holy place in Moses' tabernacle was the heavenly place of God's presence.

There were several pieces of furniture in the holy place: a table of showbread, a candlestick, and an altar of incense. But in the holy of holies, there was just one thing to look at—the Ark of the Covenant. Josephus said the design of the tabernacle was the design of heaven and earth. He said, "When Moses distinguished the tabernacle into three parts, and allowed two of them to the priests, as a place accessible and common, he denoted the land and the seas, these being of general access to all. But he set apart the third division for God because heaven is inaccessible to men."

Of course, heaven was only inaccessible in men's understanding; they thought they were separated from God. But Jesus came and revealed that heaven, or God's presence, was never inaccessible or separated from us! It was only inaccessible by the veil in men's minds!

God's Spirit has always dwelt in all men. In 1 Corinthians 3:16, Paul says, "Do you not know that you yourselves are God's temple, and the Spirit of God dwells in you?" Paul isn't just talking about a New Testament idea in this verse. In 2 Corinthians 6:16, he quotes from the Old Testament, saying, "... For we are the temple of the living God. As God has said: 'I will live with them and walk among them, and I will be their God, and they will be My people.'"

He is quoting from Exodus 29:45 and Leviticus 26:12. It seems that translators may have preferred the word 'among' instead of 'in' for these verses, possibly to suggest a distinction between God dwelling in all men and being among them.

In both verses, the Hebrew word used is *tavek*, meaning midst, within, and inside. In the Septuagint version of Leviticus 26:12, the Greek word *en* is used, meaning in. In 2 Corinthians 6:16, Paul agrees with the Septuagint, using the Greek word *en*, meaning in, when quoting these Old Testament verses: "I will live in them and walk in them." However, when translating 2 Corinthians 6:16, translators rendered both instances of *en* as 'with' and 'among.' But the truth is that He dwells in us and lives life (walks) in us! This is true in both the Old Testament and the New Testament. In fact, Paul called it the mystery of the Gospel! That mystery was hidden in the Old Testament but revealed in the New Testament.

There has never been a time that God has not dwelled in all men.

In Moses' temple, the heavenly place was God's presence, and we read in Leviticus, Exodus, and 1st and 2nd Corinthians that God's presence, or the heavenly place, dwells in men. The heavenlies in Christ is not an outside place or an "up there place" called heaven. It is in the spirit realm, in the eternal realm that is not bound by time. Eternal is always now in the spirit realm. It is not temporary or governed by time with a start and finish. It has no beginning and no end. It's in the finished work of Christ where everything is already provided for you. Eternal is in the realm of done, where we are co-seated!

The heavenly place is in us because we are in Christ and Christ is in us. The problem is that we often pray outward or upward, looking for blessings to come down from a place called heaven where we think God is. Or we believe these blessings are reserved for us someday after we die and go to heaven. But all along, all those spiritual blessings are in us, where God is, right now!

Matthew 6:21 says, "Where your treasures are, there also is your heart." What treasures? Back in verse 20, Jesus talked about the treasures in heaven. And here in verse 21, He says that those treasures are in your heart.

In Luke 6:45, it says, "A good man out of the good treasure of the heart bringeth forth that which is good." The word 'bringeth forth' is *prophero* in Greek, meaning to move something to necessary manifestation. All the treasures (every spiritual blessing) are in us, and we can bring them to necessary manifestation now! How? Not by asking God to bless us, because He already has. His blessings are a finished work in Christ.

The rest of Luke 6:45 says, "It is out of the abundance of the heart the mouth speaks." Speak out those abundances in your heart. We manifest them by speaking them forth, just as God said, "Light be" and light was brought into tangible existence. Speak out those treasures in you—all those blessings that are already yours! Do you hear the wholeness in that? All the blessings! Not some blessings, not one-by-one blessings given to us as we prove ourselves faithful. No! All blessings are in us right now.

The "all blessings" are all that He is and all that He has—His wholeness! I love that Ephesians is written from an eternal perspective, declaring to us that these truths are not time-bound. They are always right now!

Ephesians 1:4: *"For He chose us in Him before the foundation of the world to be holy and blameless in His presence in love."*

The word 'foundation' in this verse is *kataballo* instead of the usual word for a foundation, which is *themelios*. The word *kataballo* means cast down, fall away, or put in a lower place. It is not a gentle verb; it implies force and power. It is the forceful throwing down or scattering of something. Unlike *themelios*, which refers to an actual foundation in the sense of God's foundation of the world, *themelios* is used in 2 Timothy 2:19, talking about the solid foundation of God. However, the word *kataballo* implies destruction rather than construction.

So, we could translate *kataballo* or 'foundation' in Ephesians 1:4 as the fall of the world rather than God's solid foundation of the world.

The entire fall was a falling away in humanity's minds from their true identity as sons made in the image and likeness of God.

Your passage is clear and well-structured. Here is a slightly refined version for clarity and flow:

In 2 Corinthians 11:3, we read, "But I fear, lest by any means, just as the serpent beguiled Eve through his subtlety, so your minds should be corrupted from the simplicity that is in Christ." Paul is saying that Eve's mind was corrupted by the lie of the serpent, suggesting that they were not already like God. Ephesians 1:4 says that He chose us in Christ before the *kataballo*, or before the fall of the world. All humanity was secure and chosen in Christ before they were temporarily lost to a fallen mindset introduced through Adam!

It goes on to say that we should be holy and without blame before Him. The word 'before' is *katenopion*, which suggests the closest possible proximity—face-to-face with God! He chose and secured all in Christ to be intimately, fully face-to-face with Him, holy and without blame. Nothing separated us from Him except mankind's own imagination. The fall didn't change who we were created to be, and it didn't change God's opinion of us.

Ephesians 1:5-6 says, *"Having predestined us to adoption as sons by Jesus Christ to Himself, according to the good pleasure of His will, ⁶ to the praise of the glory of His grace, by which He made us accepted in the Beloved."*

I love the fullness message of these verses 4–6—the fullness of who we are right now and who mankind has always been eternally in Christ. It declares that all of this—the fullness of who we are in Him —He made us in love! This is the wonderful, glorious, eternal good news of His great love for us!

- Verse 3 — Fully blessed!
- Verse 4 — Fully chosen! Fully holy! Fully blameless! Fully spotless!
- Verse 5 — Fully sons! Fully heirs!
- And verse 6 — Fully graced and fully loved!

I love these verses in the Mirror Bible:*"He associated us IN Christ before the fall of the world! Jesus is God's mind made up about us! He always knew in His love that he would present us again face-to-face before him in blameless innocence. ⁵ He is the architect of our design; His heart dream realized our coming of age IN Christ. ⁶ His grace-plan is to be celebrated: He greatly endeared us and highly favored us IN Christ. His love for His Son is His love for us."*

So, how do we know our physical body is as fully redeemed as our spirit? How do we know that we are whole and complete right now? Romans 8:11 says, "The Spirit of Christ quickened or gave life to our physical body."

> The Mirror Bible says it this way, *"Our union with Christ further reveals that because the same Spirit that awakened the body of Jesus from the dead inhabits us, we equally participate in His resurrection. In the same act of authority whereby God raised Jesus from the dead, He co-restores your body to life by his indwelling Spirit. (Your body need never again be an excuse for an inferior expression of the Christ-life, just as it was reckoned dead in Christ's death, it is now reckoned alive in his resurrection.)"*

His life flows through our entire being—our spirit, mind, emotions, will, and physical body—because our body was co-restored with His! In the last chapter, I told you that when Jesus touched the leper, his body was altered and transformed—he was made whole. How much more, then, does His life flowing through our entire being alter and transform every part of us!

If that's true, why aren't we experiencing a transformed, redeemed physical body? Because we don't expect it. We were told that the glorification and redemption of our physical bodies would take place after we die and go to a place called heaven someday. We've been taught that sickness and disease are a normal part of life and to be expected, and that aging and our bodies breaking down is how we were created to live here on earth. Because we believe this, it becomes our reality, shaping our experiences in life. Consequently, our lives are lived in this distorted reality, driven by our experiences and the opinions we've accepted as truth.

> But the good news is that you may be just one thought and one confession away from the tangible manifestation—don't quit now!

Confession has gotten a bad rap over the years, but 'confession' is *homologeo*. It is from two words: *homou* meaning 'together,' and *lego* meaning 'to speak to a conclusion.' Confession is simply co-speaking with God, speaking forth His conclusions about us. Unfortunately, we have listened to other voices and spoken their conclusions about us—voices such as sickness, disease, or age. Age is just a number! But for most of us, the number of our age wars against us in our minds, telling us we're old and what we should expect—sickness, a slowing body, decreased mental and visual acuity, and impending physical death.

However, God says, "As He is, so are we in this world—right now!" He is immortal—we are immortal. He is the health and wholeness of our bodies—so we are whole, 100% filled with divine health.

Don't let the false appearance of sickness and disease dictate what you think and speak. Co-speak with God—declare His conclusions about you. He is the health of your body and the source of your life. You are fully redeemed, fully whole, fully filled with the Godhead! This is a right-now conclusion—not someday after we die.

Death is not our savior! Death has no say in our life. It is a defeated enemy that enslaved men until the cross. They lived powerless to death and sin. We are not powerless in life—we are masters of all!

We barely scratched the surface in these few verses of Ephesians! But I hope it helped you grasp who you are in Christ—whole and complete, lacking nothing! I encourage you to study it further and deepen your understanding of these truths, making them a part of your thoughts, your confession, and your expectation!

Chapter 3

Ephesians One – Eternal Redemption

"In Him we have redemption through His blood, the forgiveness of sins, according to the riches of His grace [8] which He made to abound toward us in all wisdom and prudence, [9] having made known to us the mystery of His will, according to His good pleasure which He purposed in Himself, [10] that in the dispensation of the fullness of the times He might gather together in one all things in Christ, both which are in heaven and which are on earth — in Him."

Ephesians 1:7-10 (NKJV)

I n verse 7, it says, *"In whom we have redemption through His blood, the forgiveness of sins, according to the riches of His grace."* When we read that verse, we need to remember that God's plan of redemption has always been an eternal plan. It was not a reaction to Adam's fall. Jesus was never God's plan B.

In the previous chapter, we explored verses 1–6 and discovered a purpose and plan older than time itself. God brought this eternal plan into reality when He created mankind. He made them in His image and likeness, granting them dominion over all things. Despite what many believe, Adam and mankind never lost God's image, likeness, or their dominion on earth. Instead, they began living life ruled by their carnal, fleshly understanding, forgetting who they truly were and becoming dominated by the sense realm.

> Deuteronomy 32:18 says, "Of the Rock who begot you, you are unmindful and have forgotten the God who fathered you."

> And Isaiah in 51:1 says, "Listen to Me, you who pursue righteousness, you who seek the LORD: Look to the rock from which you were cut, and to the quarry from which you were hewn."

They were striving for something they already were. Humanity has always been the image and likeness of God, even when living out of alignment with Him and with a false, distorted sense of identity. Remember, Paul started this letter by telling us who we were before the foundation of the world.

The term 'foundation' in this context, *kataballo*, actually refers to the fall, not God's creation foundation, as we saw in the last chapter. Paul is telling us who we were before the fall—before humanity adopted a fallen mindset. This does not imply that mankind's nature changed after the fall! Mankind has always been beloved sons in the image and likeness of Abba. The fall didn't change that! The fall couldn't change our nature because we were secure and chosen in Christ, and He was the Lamb slain before the *kataballo*—before the fall!

So, with that in mind, let's go back to verse 4 for a minute: "Just as He chose us in Him before the foundation of the world, that we should be holy and without blame before Him in love." The word 'chose' is *eklego* in Greek. It comes from two words: *ek*, meaning source or origin, and *lego*, meaning logic or original thought. It is to communicate an idea and to speak its conclusion. It says we were chosen. He is our Source and Origin. We came from Him. We are the expression of His original thought, His blueprint design. What was His original thought or blueprint design regarding mankind? Made in His image and likeness with dominion over all the works of His hands.

This is who we are and always have been—chosen in Him, coming from Him, and the expression of His original thought. We were made in His image and likeness with all power and dominion in the earth.

Then it says we should be holy and without blame before Him in love. In Greek, it doesn't say "should be." It says "to be holy and without blame before Him in love." The word 'be' is *eimi*, meaning to exist, or "I AM." It is in the present infinitive tense, which suggests a continual engagement on our part. We read the phrase "should be" and interpret it as though we are not yet holy and without blame. We think it means we should be, but we're not yet! In our estimation, we aren't living up to God's ideal of being holy and without blame. But it's not saying we should be, in the sense that hopefully someday we'll reach that ideal.

It's stating that we are holy and blameless—without fault—before Him in love. And we are to continually embrace and live out this understanding!

How? By agreeing with Abba, "Yes Abba, I am right now holy and without blame." When you first start doing that, you might hear that little accusing voice in your head saying, "Really? Do you remember what you did last month, last week, or even last night?" Again, continually engage by agreeing with Him, "Yes Abba, I am holy and blameless because I AM is Holy and Blameless in me!" I promise you, that accusing voice will eventually become silent!

I used to read verse 7 ("we have redemption through His blood and forgiveness of sins") and view it as God's response to the fall, to human failure. In other words, God's plan B. As in, because of the fall, something needed to be done, so Jesus stepped in, relating it only to the historical event of the cross. But going back to verses 4 and 5, Paul already established that this all took place before the foundation of the world—before the fall, not as a response to it.

Remember, verses 3–14 comprise one long, run-on sentence or one continuous thought from an eternal perspective! Paul is talking about our eternal identity IN Christ, not our identity after the cross. In other words, God chose us according to His good pleasure, not because He fixed man's sin or fall. Verses 4 and 5 say, "He chose us in Christ and predestined us in sonship according to His good pleasure, in love!"

And in Him, we have redemption and forgiveness. This isn't based upon a historical event. It is because we were chosen before the foundation of the world according to the riches of His grace.

We've looked at things like redemption, forgiveness, holiness, and righteousness and thought it was non-existent before the cross.

But Paul, here in Ephesians, is telling us these things were eternal realities, they were never bound by time. Jesus fleshed out in time and space what was eternal. Don't forget He is the Lamb slain before the foundation or the fall.

The Old Testament tells us that God was *Yahweh Rapha* before the cross, before Jesus bore the stripes two thousand years ago. We've translated that as He is the Lord our Healer. But in Hebrew, it is I AM your Health, or I AM your Wholeness. Jesus told the Pharisees before Abraham was, I AM existed. Jesus Christ, the Great I AM, and ALL His FINISHED works are ETERNAL!

His bearing the stripes was the revealing of what had always been. Revealing what was before the foundation of the world or before the fall. Forgiveness of sins isn't something that just happened when Jesus went to the Cross—because Jesus didn't go to the cross for man's failure. He went to the cross to reveal Abba's unchanging, offensive, beautiful love for all His sons.

Becoming the *final* sacrifice to end the sacrifices that Abba never desired or required and doing away with sin, death, and all of the old Adam.

Verse 9 says, "Having made known unto us the mystery of His will." Verses 9 and 10 are so good in the Mirror Bible: "The secret is out! His cherished love dream now unfolds in front of our very eyes ⟨10⟩ In the economy of the fullness of time, everything culminates IN Christ. All that is in heaven and all that is on earth is reconciled IN Him. Jesus is the consummation of the ages."

In the historical event of His incarnation, from His virgin birth to His being seated at the right hand of the Father, He did not come to give us something that was not already ours. But instead revealed them to us and showed us that this is who we were created to be before the foundation of the world.

Colossians 1:26 says, *"The mystery of the Gospel, Christ in us, has been hidden from ages and generations but is now manifest to His saints."*

The word 'saint' does not mean people who go to church. It means sacred ones; all those who are sacred to God. Who was sacred to God? ALL mankind! John 3:16 says, *"For God so loved the world!"* The good news that was hidden from ages and generations has now been revealed to His sacred ones. It is the unveiling, the revelation of something that was always true but was lost.

What was the mystery hidden? It was Christ IN us, the hope of Glory. Paul is saying that what has been from before the foundations of the world, Christ IN you, is NOW manifested to ALL mankind! The word 'manifest' is *phaneroó* and means made clear, made plain. The mystery of Christ IN us has become apparent. It's become graspable! Mankind has always had the life of God IN them. But after the fall, they forgot who they were. Deuteronomy 32:18 says that "You are unmindful of the Rock who begot you and have forgotten the God who fathered you." In other words, they had forgotten they were sons!

2 Timothy 1:9-10 says, *"Who has saved us and called us with a holy calling, not according to our works, but according to His own purpose and grace which was given to us IN Christ Jesus before time began, ¹⁰ but has now been revealed by the appearing of our Savior Jesus Christ, who has abolished death and brought life and immortality to light through the gospel."*

We were not saved and called with a holy calling according to our works. And it had nothing to do with a response to man's failure or fall. His saving us was not a response to Adam's fall, but it was according to His own purpose and grace. He saved us before the fall! Our salvation is an eternal truth, an eternal reality.

Don't let the word 'saved' throw you. We think of the term saved as merely being forgiven of sins and making it to heaven someday and missing hell. And we think we received it because of our response to

Jesus — praying a prayer and asking Him to come to live in our hearts. But the word 'saved' is *sozo* and means delivered, healed, prospered, whole and complete. It means undamaged and unbroken.

We were saved—we were whole in Christ—before time began.

In verse 10, it says, "But now is made manifest (or revealed) by the appearing of our Savior Jesus Christ!" His appearing was not to save us or make us holy but to reveal (to make manifest, or to make clear, plain, and graspable) the Father's love and purpose before time began. We thought the Gospel was subject to the appearing. In other words, when Jesus appeared, then the Gospel was brought to earth. No, the Gospel was what the appearing confirmed! The gospel of grace has always existed. It's *eternal*! It was never bound by time. And it wasn't a response to the fall.

The fall didn't change God's mind about us! We were still who He said we were! And we still had all that He said we had.

In 1 Peter 1:18-20, it says, *"Knowing that you were not redeemed with perishable things like silver or*

*gold from your futile way of life inherited from
your forefathers, [19] but with precious blood, as of a
lamb unblemished and spotless, the blood of
Christ. [20] For He was foreknown before the foundation of the world but has appeared in these last
times for the sake of you."*

Verse 18 in the NKJV says, *"From your aimless conduct received by
tradition from your fathers."* The phrase 'received by tradition' in
Greek is *patroparadotas*, meaning something passed on by fathers or
traditions passed down from ancestors. It was the traditional way of
doing something. Remember Deuteronomy 32:18 tells us they had
forgotten God was their Father. They forgot they were sons made in
the image and likeness of Abba with ALL dominion. Instead, they
lived life experiencing the things their ancestors experienced.
Ephesians 1:5 says, "We were predestined (before the foundation of
the world) as sons."

Hebrews 4:3 says, *"For we who have believed do enter
into rest as He has said as I have sworn in My
wrath if they shall enter into My rest although the
works were finished before the foundation of the
world."*

All was FINISHED before the foundation of the world (*kataballo*).
Jesus came and revealed that there is a FINISHED rest that we can
experience. And it was given before the foundation of the world or
before the fall. The incarnation of Jesus revealed what had become a

mystery to man when he fell in his understanding of who he was as a son in Abba's image and likeness.

We have always been whole—blessed; chosen; holy; blameless; spotless; sons; heirs; graced; loved; forgiven; and redeemed. And our redemption was an eternal redemption that was revealed in time and restored to us through the incarnation of Jesus!

Chapter 4

Sons & Heirs

W here we have erred was in making these eternal truths time-sensitive. Abba said it took place before the realm of time, before the fall, from eternity past. Jesus willingly went to the cross, not to bring about what was always true of man, but to reveal what is eternally true of man. And we are to rest not just in what He FINISHED two thousand years ago, of course, it includes that, but our rest is in the understanding that it was FINISHED before the foundation of the world.

Ephesians 1:11 says, *"Being predestined according to the purpose of him who worketh all things after the counsel of His own will."* And Isaiah 46:10 says, *"Declaring the end from the beginning and from the ancient times the things not yet done, saying My counsel shall stand, and I will do all My pleasure."*

The word 'declaring' is derived from the Hebrew term *nagad*, which means not only to declare but also to stand boldly opposite. The first instance of *nagad* appears in Genesis when God questioned Adam, 'Who told (*nagad*) you that you were naked?' Here, Adam's self-perception starkly contrasts with what Abba had originally revealed about his identity—whole and complete in Him. God's declaration of the end from the beginning boldly opposes what may appear accurate in our lives or in the world. It counters the declarations that people may make about themselves or about Him. This declaration of the end is firmly rooted in the beginning, in what He proclaimed about mankind before time began, before humanity was even created.

God's declaration of the end is rooted in the beginning declaration, in what He had said about mankind before time began before man was ever created.

Genesis 1:26 recounts the moment when God (*Elohim*: Father, Son, and Holy Spirit) declared, 'Let Us make man in Our image and according to Our likeness so that they will have dominion over all things.' This proclamation encapsulated God's vision for mankind's nature and destiny. Despite Adam's belief that he was naked and stripped of God's nature and authority, God's declaration remained steadfast. Adam was still whole and complete in Him, created in His image and likeness. What does it mean to be in God's image and likeness? We are a reflection of love, holiness, righteousness, goodness, and more. Even as mankind continued from Adam, feeling separated from God, His original declaration endured. This foundational declaration would determine our destiny, continuing to define all humanity regardless of their self-perception.

Jesus came and unveiled what had always been true of us from God's perspective.

First Peter 1:18-20 tells us that Jesus was foreknown before the foundation of the world. He was revealed for their sakes to redeem them from their futile way of life inherited from their fathers, or from their aimless conduct received by the traditions of their ancestors. In other words, they were redeemed from following their ancestors' ways of doing things—redeemed from not living life as sons in the image and likeness of Abba, as lords in the earth. Jesus revealed to us what living as a son from before the fall looked like.

And as He is, so are we—sons and heirs, lords of the earth, from before creation!

God said in Isaiah, "My counsel (my purpose) shall stand, and I will do ALL My pleasure." Paul echoes this in Ephesians 1:5 stating that, "He predestined us as sons according to His good pleasure and will." Sons made in His image and likeness. Initially, in Genesis 1, God affirms that we were made in His image and likeness. However, after the fall, in Genesis 5:3, when Adam was 130, it's noted that he had a son in his own likeness, in his own image. It's intriguing how the words 'image' and 'likeness' are reversed here, perhaps reflecting

Adam's confusion and distorted identity in his own mind. This false, corrupted sense of self was then passed on to his son.

Colossians 1:21 describes how 'Mankind was once alienated and hostile or adversaries in their minds,' while 2 Corinthians 11:3 portrays Paul's concern about our minds being corrupted away from the singleness and blamelessness in Christ, likening it to the serpent deceiving Eve. Adam and Eve's corrupted minds led them to declare about themselves that they lacked something of God's identity within them, deviating from the truth that they were already like God. Nevertheless, God has declared the end from the beginning.

Our origin is not rooted in Adam's declaration from the fall, but solely in what God declared from the beginning, before creation.

Ephesians 1:5 reveals that His good pleasure predestined us to sonship through Jesus Christ. The term 'predestined' signifies being marked out beforehand; predetermined boundaries set for us before creation. Our sonship was established, predetermined before creation. Furthermore, He assured that His purposes, His counsel, will stand for eternity! The term 'good pleasure' stems from *eudokeo* in Greek, derived from *eu* meaning good and *dokeo* meaning the original thought or opinion.

What was Abba's original good thought?

In Genesis 1:26, we hear His declaration: 'Let us make man in our image and likeness,' and in Genesis 1:31, we read, 'And God saw everything that He had made, and behold, it was very good. And the evening and the morning were the sixth day.' Then He rested! His rest signified that everything was indeed VERY GOOD—all was FINISHED. He rested because He knew His counsel and purpose would stand! He declared the end from the beginning, and the fall could never change that. His purpose would stand, and He would fulfill all His pleasure, with neither Adam's mistakes and failures nor ours ever altering that truth!

All mankind are beloved sons, created in His image and likeness, endowed with dominion over all things

This was His purpose and good pleasure concerning us. The writer of Hebrews tells us that Jesus brought many (all) sons to glory. The word 'brought' is *ago* in Greek, meaning to lead to rest. And the root of the word 'glory' is *dokeo*, meaning original thought or opinion. Jesus led all of Abba's sons (all humanity) to be able to rest in Abba's original thought and very good opinion that they were beloved sons made in His image and likeness, with all dominion.

His original thought of us stands firm. He declared the end from the beginning before creation. Who we are and what we have was predetermined and set before time began!

- We were chosen in Him before the foundation of the world (Ephesians 1:4)
- We were predestined as sons before creation (Ephesians 1:5)
- We were saved and called with a holy calling before the world began (2 Timothy 1:9)
- We were justified and glorified (Romans 8:30)
- And we have obtained an inheritance (Ephesians 1:11)

The first part of Ephesians 1:11 says, "In Him also we have obtained an inheritance." This verse is all God! It was in Him, He predestined it, and it was according to His purpose and the counsel of His will that we have obtained this inheritance. The word 'obtained' is an aorist indicative passive tense, indicating a past tense fact—a FINISHED work. And it's in the passive voice, meaning nothing is required on our part. We had nothing to do with obtaining it—it's fully ours because of what He FINISHED.

We're not waiting on our inheritance in the sweet by and by or when we prove ourselves good stewards and worthy of all He has for us. No! Our inheritance is in Him, and He is in us. Therefore, we have all we will ever need inside us.

Second Peter 1:3 says, "His divine power has given us all things that pertain to life and godliness." Ephesians 1:11 tells us that this inheritance we obtained was predestined—it was marked out and established for us before time began. According to the purpose of the One who works all things according to the counsel of His will. The word 'counsel' in Greek is boule, signifying a resolved plan. It's about planning with complete determination or a firm decision of a course of action. It's a powerful word, emphasizing the predetermined intention driving the planning. Synonyms of resolve include firm, fixed, decided, and concluded. What I hear in that is 'It is finished!'"

C. BAXTER KRUGER, IN HIS BOOK, *JESUS AND THE UNDOING OF ADAM*:

"The response of the Father, Son and Spirit to Adam's plunge into utter ruin can be put into one word: 'No!' In that 'No' echoes the eternal 'Yes' of the Trinity to us. Creation flows out of the circle of divine sharing and out of the decision, the determined decision, to share the Triune life with human beings. That will of God for our blessing that determined 'Yes' to us translates into an intolerable 'No!' in the teeth of the Fall. God is for us and therefore opposed—utterly, eternally, and passionately opposed—to our destruction. That opposition, that fiery and passionate and determined 'No!' to the disaster of the Fall, is the proper understanding of the wrath of God. Wrath is not the opposite of love. Wrath is the love of God in action, in opposing action. It is precisely because the Triune God has spoken an eternal 'Yes!' to the human race, a 'Yes!' to life and fullness and joy for us, that the Fall and its disaster is met with a stout and intolerable 'No! This is not acceptable. I did not create you for misery.' Therein the plan of reconciliation begins to unfold."

Our inheritance was determined before creation—it has always been ours in Him from before time began. And what Abba determined always stood firm. The fall didn't change what was eternally pre-determined for us as sons. We were predestined (established before creation) to adoption—sonship. In other words, we have always been sons before creation, before the fall, and after the fall.

Adoption means being placed as sons. Sonship and inheritance go together. In Luke 15:31, the father said to his son, "All that I have is yours." And in Galatians 4:1, it says, "Now I say, 'That the heir, as long as he is a child, differs nothing from a servant, though he be master of all.'" The son is the heir. He is the master of all, but he's still a child (verse 3) in bondage under the elements of the law. The word 'child' is *nepias* in Greek and means the non-speaking, the infant, the immature, and simple-minded. This is who man was in bondage to the elements of the law. Paul says, under the Law, you were an infant, immature, simple-minded, and non-speaking. In other words, under the Law, their words were unable to produce the authority they were intended to produce in their life.

He's talking to the Jews who had been under the Law before the cross. Not us!

Because the good news of the gospel is, we were never under the law. And after the cross, no one is under the law. From Abba's perspective, all mankind are sons, not immature children. However, when we fall under the "do to become", or the "if and then" language of the Law, we don't walk in our God-given authority with the power to be able to administer all our rightful inheritance. We are unable to enjoy and walk in the fullness of what is ours in Christ. Even though we are masters of all. And as masters of all, as sons and heirs, we have been given absolute control over the outcome of the events of our lives.

That means that we are the master of our own destiny in Him—not apart from Him. It's in Him, it's because of what He's FINISHED that we are masters of all!

Psalm 8:4-6 says, *"What is man, that thou art mindful of him? and the son of man, that thou visitest him?* [5] *For thou hast made him a little lower than the angels, and hast crowned him with glory and honor.* [6] *Thou madest him to have dominion over the works of thy hands; thou hast put all things under his feet."*

In Hebrew, it doesn't say 'a little lower than angels.' It says 'a little lower than Elohim,' meaning a little lower than Father, Son, and Spirit. We were crowned with glory and honor, given dominion over all the works of God's hands. And all things have been put under our feet. All means all! Hebrews 2:8 reiterates this: 'YOU HAVE PUT EVERYTHING IN SUBJECTION UNDER HIS FEET. For in subjecting all things to him, He left nothing that is not subject to him.' We are masters of all—sons and heirs!

Yet, many still fall short of experiencing this inheritance we have in Christ. Why? Because we haven't understood that He finished all! Many people are still seeking to appease God through their behavior, still waiting for God to bless them, still waiting to become who they already are. Most are living under an 'if and then,' or a 'do to become' mindset with God. In other words, if I do this, then God will bless me, give me more favor, anointing, abundance, healing, etc.

We must grasp the reality that IT IS FINISHED!
We are sons who rule and reign in a finished life!

Christ fully redeemed us. He freed us by reviving us. The word 'reviving' refers to what was already alive at one time but lost its breath—it was RE-vived. What man lost was not his sonship, the nature of God, or his dominion over all things. What he lost was the knowledge or revelation of his sonship and dominion, which consequently led to the loss of all things.

Jesus RE-vived in us the revelation of our sonship and dominion and restored ALL the resources of our inheritance to us.

The word 'adoption' in this context differs significantly from our Western concept of adoption. It does not imply bringing someone into a family that was not originally theirs. Instead, adoption as sons was a Greek and Roman cultural rite of passage from childhood to adulthood. In the context of what Paul is discussing here, it signifies the transition from living under the Law to grace. Under the Law, they were children, but under grace, they become mature, adult sons. It was the father who determined the timing of this transition.

We often think that maturing as sons is a process, but the father decided when the child would be placed as a son, transitioning into a mature son with full inheritance rights. When that time came, the son was brought face-to-face with the father.

Galatians 4:5-6 says, *"But when the fullness of time had come, God sent forth His Son, born of woman, born under the law, ⁵ To redeem those who were under the law, so that we might receive adoption as sons."*

Luke 5:24 says, "For this son of mine was dead and is alive again (revived); he was lost and is found. And they began to be merry (to rejoice; to have a cheery state of mind because of the feeling of victory)."

What was the son dead to? The revelation of his sonship. In Luke 15:21, the son says, "I have sinned against heaven and before you; no longer am I worthy to be called your son. Make me as one of your hired servants." He had a sin consciousness that made him feel unworthy of being his father's son because of his wrong actions.

But the father ignored the son's words and spoke to his servants to quickly bring out the best robe, clothe him, and give him a ring for his hand and sandals for his feet! The father knows the difference between his son and his servants, even if the son does not yet. The word 'quickly' is *tachu*, meaning speedily, without delay, immediately! There was no delay, no hesitation on the father's part. His son was restored immediately to enjoy his full inheritance right away.

The robe, or toga, is *verillus*, meaning the cloak of manhood or the cloak of mature sonship. The robe declared the son an adult, a mature son fully able to administer his inheritance. From that point on, all the father's estate belonged to the father and him jointly. It was a joint inheritance; they were co-heirs. The ring allowed him to fully administer all the inheritance. It was the sign of authority that said he was the master of all, just like the father. The sandals identified him as a son, not a servant, because only sons wore sandals.

Under grace, we're all recognized and acknowledged as adult, mature sons—not as children with no authority over our Father's estate.

We often refer to new believers as baby Christians, implying a growing-up process of sonship. But that's not what the Father said. This 'growing up process' is our idea, not Abba's. He says we have all received the adoption as sons. What we think of as a 'growing up process' is simply awakening to the understanding that we have always been mature sons. We just didn't know it. It is agreeing with what Abba knows to be true about us. All are face-to-face with the Father in Christ, and all were declared mature sons and heirs, with full, unlimited access to manage their inheritance! Galatians 4:7 says, 'Wherefore thou art no more a servant (child), but a son; and if (or because) a son, also an heir through (*dia* – completely, successfully through) God.'

The prodigal son, from our perspective, appears immature and hasn't been a good steward of his inheritance. But there was no process—no proving time required by the father. Not even when he asked for it upon returning home, requesting to prove himself as a servant. We've made receiving our inheritance about going through a process of passing tests and trials before we are entrusted by the Father with anything (such as favor, anointing, prosperity, etc.). But Ephesians 1:11 says, 'In Him we have obtained an inheritance.' It's a past-tense fact—finished!"

There is no *proving time* needed to receive it. It's already ours. All we need to do is awaken to who we are, and what is ours, and walk in that revelation.

In Galatians 4:9, Paul addresses these believing Galatians about their new life in Christ. He says, 'But now after you have known God, or rather are known by God.' At first glance, it sounds like Paul is correcting himself. However, the word 'rather' means far more, or to a greater degree. Paul isn't correcting himself. He's emphasizing that while they now know God, they are far more known by Him—known from before creation!

The Mirror Bible says it like this, *"In the meantime, you have come to know the real God* (quite unlike the god of your imagination); **what is most significant, however, is to discover that He knew you all along!"**

Thank God our sonship and inheritance don't depend on our ability to know God. And yet, that is the very thing that has been taught as a form of law in the church. Teaching that, to the degree that you know God "you will then be able to ...." That's another form of legalism putting people in performance mode... in an "if and then" mindset!

But the truth is we are known by Him as sons and heirs... free IN Christ! Free from the bondage of "do to become", of "if and then." FINISHED!

Paul's entire message in Ephesians is about how intimately God has known us and provided for us from before the foundation of the world. God (Father, Son, and Spirit) says about you, 'It is FINISHED! You are perfect, complete, lacking nothing—whole!'

It's time to wake up to what God has always known about you, walk in it, and *be* the person He created you to be!

Chapter 5

Jehovah Rapha

Wholeness is our inheritance, and part of being whole is living in abundant or divine health all the time. However, too often we live by our experiences with sickness and disease rather than from what God says is true about us and who He is in us. We've come to treat sickness and disease as normal occurrences in our lives instead of seeing them as defeated on the cross when Jesus overcame death. He is Jehovah or *Yahweh Rapha*, the Lord our Health, or the Lord our Wholeness. This was meant to be our daily experience in life.

> Romans 15:4 says, *"For whatever things were written before were written for our learning that we through patience and comfort of the Scriptures might have hope."*

Paul says that whatever things were written before were written for our learning. What is he talking about? He's referring to the Old Testament writings. He is saying that whatever was written in the Old Testament was for our teaching and instruction. Then he goes on to tell us why: so that through the endurance and encouragement of the Scriptures, we might have hope. The New Testament word for 'hope' in Greek is *elpis* and means confident expectation. Paul is saying that the things written in the Old Testament were meant to instruct us, so we might develop a confident expectation of living a victorious, successful life of wholeness in every area.

In 1 Corinthians 10:11, it says, *"Now all these things happened to them as examples, and they were written for our admonition, upon whom the ends of the ages have come. The things that happened to Israel were examples written for our admonition."*

The word 'admonition' means instruction, placing of the mind, or instruction for the mind. The events that happened to Israel were written to shape our mindset; they were intended to instruct our minds today to develop an expectation of wholeness in our experiences in this life. However, we must establish some parameters for interpretation before delving into the Old Testament. Otherwise, we risk getting pulled back into the law, legalism, and the revival of Judaic practices that were never meant for us. This is the very issue Paul addressed in Galatians and the writer of Hebrews also discussed. Therefore, we must set some guidelines for studying the Old Testament to learn from it.

In 1 Peter 1:10-12 it says, *"Of which salvation the
prophets have inquired and searched diligently,
who prophesied **of the grace** that should come
unto you: *11* Searching what, or what manner of
time the Spirit of Christ which was in them did
signify when it testified beforehand the sufferings
of Christ, **and the glory** that should follow *12*
Unto whom it was revealed, that not unto them
selves, but unto us, they did minister the things,
which are now reported unto you by them that
have preached **the gospel** unto you with the
Holy Ghost sent down from heaven, which things
the angels desire to look into."*

These verses provide good filters for interpreting Old Testament
Scriptures. We should extract from the Old Testament writings the
grace, glory (which is the view and opinion of God, the nature, and
acts of God in manifestation), and everything included in the good
news of the Gospel of Jesus Christ. Anything that does not reveal
these aspects should be left in the Old Testament and not brought
forward into our understanding. Because it was never meant to
instruct us or give us a confident expectation of living victoriously

Ephesians 1:7 says, 'In Him we have redemption, forgiveness of our
sins, through the shedding of His blood.' And just four verses later, in
verse 11, it states, 'In Him also we have obtained an inheritance.' So,
not only have we been redeemed, but we have also obtained an inheritance. Understanding our practical experience of this inheritance
begins with a revelation of Israel's exodus from Egypt. When they left

Egypt, what were they heading for? Their inheritance. In this way, their redemption serves as a picture of our own redemption.

We're also going to look at four types and shadows in the Old Testament story of the exodus. Types and shadows were prophetic pictures of things to come.

---

1. Pharaoh — He was the hard taskmaster, the one who did not know Joseph. He is a type of Satan in the Old Testament. Ezekiel 29 refers to this pharaoh as the great monster or great serpent. Not all previous pharaohs were a type of Satan, just this one. Some pharaohs were friends of Abraham, and at least one was a friend of Joseph. But this Pharaoh, he represents Satan or the adversary.

2. Egypt — A type of sin. This refers to the fallen, distorted mindset, not the behaviors we typically call "sins."

3. Egyptians — A type of death. Death here refers to more than the cessation of life, either spiritual or physical. It encompasses all the attributes of death — sickness, disease, poverty, addiction, etc. These are the results of sin (the fallen, distorted sense of identity) entering the world.

4. Red Sea — A type of the blood of Jesus.

Romans 5:12 says, 'Therefore, just as through one man sin entered the world, and death through sin, and thus death spread to all men because all sinned.' Sin came through one man. Who is the man Paul was referring to? Adam. Notice it says death came through sin. So, apart from sin, there is no death. Sin and death have a cause-and-effect relationship: sin is the cause, and death is the effect. Then it says death spread to all men because all sinned. Death and its attributes—sickness, disease, poverty, fear, etc.—spread to all men. The word 'spread' is *dierchomai*, meaning to spread as a report.

1 Peter 1:18 says, *"Knowing that you were redeemed from your futile manner of life handed down from your fathers, not by perishable things — by silver or by gold."*

Futile manner refers to an unproductive, ineffective, unreal manner of life. The phrase 'handed down' is *patroparadotos*in Greek, meaning the traditions handed down from forefathers. In other words, their traditional ways of doing and believing were passed down from generation to generation. Death and its attributes—sickness, disease, poverty, etc.—spread to all men. Generation after generation, they passed on their experiences with death and all that came with it: sickness, disease, poverty, and more.

We do the same thing today. If our grandparents or parents had a disease, we often expect to have it too. As a result, disease, poverty, failure, fear, and similar conditions are passed down to future generations as normal experiences of life. These negative experiences continue from generation to generation until we choose to think differently—until we choose not to let someone else's experiences dictate our lives and refuse to allow these distorted mindsets to persist in our thinking. Thus, death and its effects—sickness, disease, poverty, fear—spread as a report from generation to generation. They entered the world through sin. Sin was the cause, and death was the effect. But the effect only exists as long as the cause persists.

Remove the cause, and the effects are also automatically removed.

The term 'exodus' literally means going out. Their exodus out of Egypt was written to shape our understanding. So, what is it about the story of Israel's exodus that is meant to instruct our minds? It is to teach us about the grace, glory, and the good news of Jesus Christ bringing all mankind out of sin and death two thousand years ago.

The Red Sea is a type of the blood of Jesus, which signifies the FINISHED work of Christ. It stood as an impassable barrier between Egypt (a type of sin) and the people of God, creating a separation between sin and God's people.

In Exodus 15, the children of Israel have just come out of the Red Sea, and it says in verses 22–26, "So, Moses brought Israel from the Red Sea; then they went out into the Wilderness of Shur. And they went three days in the wilderness and found no water [23] Now when they came to Marah, they could not drink the waters of Marah, for they were bitter. Therefore, the name of it was called Marah. [24] and the people complained against Moses, saying, 'what shall we drink?' [25] So, he cried out to the LORD, and the LORD showed him a tree. When he cast it into the waters, the waters were made sweet. There He made a statute and an ordinance for them, and there He tested them, [26] and said, 'if you diligently heed the voice of the LORD your God and do what is right in His sight and give ear to His commandments and keep an eye on His statutes, I will put none of the diseases on you which I have brought on the Egyptians. For I AM the LORD who heals you.'"

We will deal with a lot in these verses, but first, let's look at verse 26a. It says, "...and said if you diligently heed the voice of the LORD your God and do what is right in His sight and give ear to His commandments and keep an eye on His statutes, I will put none of the diseases on you which I have brought on the Egyptians. For I AM the LORD who heals you."

The first and most important thing to understand about this verse is that these are not conditions required of you to be healed or made whole. These conditions were fulfilled by Jesus for you and as you.

No one could have fulfilled those conditions—only Jesus. I say this because some make healing conditional based on this verse, treating it as an 'if and then' promise of God. **But Jesus fulfilled these conditions two thousand years ago.** He diligently heeded the voice of the Lord God, did what was right in His sight, gave ear to His commandments, and kept all His statutes. And seriously, thank God we don't have to do it, because if healing were conditional, no one would ever get healed! But the good news is that healing isn't conditional upon anything—it's a FINISHED work!

Now, with that understanding, we can go on and look at the rest of verse 26. It says, "~~I will put none of the diseases on you which I have brought on the Egyptians.~~ For I AM the LORD who heals you." As for the part that says, "I will put none of the diseases on you which I have brought on the Egyptians," we're not going to bring that forward in our understanding. We're going to leave it in the Old Testament. In fact, you can simply cross it out, like I did. Remember, we're only pulling out the grace, glory, and the good news of Jesus Christ. So, all we want to focus on in this part of verse 26 is 'For I am the LORD who heals you.' The word 'for' means 'because'. In other words, it says, 'because I am the LORD who heals you.'

The first thing I want you to see in this last part of verse 26 is that God makes an association or **a connection between disease and Egypt (a type of sin).** He says I will put none of the diseases on you which I have brought on the Egyptians. For I am the LORD who heals you.

Let's look at Deuteronomy 7, and then we'll come back to Exodus 15. Deuteronomy 7:15 says, 'And the LORD will take away from you all sickness and will afflict you with none of these terrible diseases of

Egypt which you have known.' The word 'of' establishes a possessive relationship between disease and Egypt. Diseases are *of* Egypt. Then He says, 'Which you have known.' So, they were familiar with the diseases *of* Egypt.

What is Egypt a type of? It is a type of sin—the fallen condition of mankind's minds. We're not talking about behaviors the church has labeled as sin.

The second thing we notice in this part of the verse is that He says, 'because I am Jehovah (*Yahweh*) Rapha!' That word 'because' is important for us to understand. We've translated this verse as He is the Lord who heals us. And that's an acceptable translation, except that it suggests the continuing need for healing. In other words, we read it as I am the Lord who heals you, and we take that to mean that every time we get sick, He will heal us. And, of course, that's true. He will heal us because He loves us, and He always meets us where we're at.

But that's not what He wanted us to understand from those words. We are supposed to grasp the permanency of being healed and whole because we're no longer associated with Egypt (a type of sin)—we've been redeemed!

Just as Israel was fully redeemed from Egypt, we've been fully redeemed from sin!

This verse would be better understood as: I AM your perpetual Health, or I AM your perpetual Wholeness! This verse is not about something He does, like healing us, but instead, it is about who He is: the Lord our perpetual, never-ending Health and Wholeness! Because of who He is, He does what He does. The Psalmist in Psalm 119:68 said, "You are good, and you do good." He does good because He is good. He heals and makes whole because He is our never-ending Health and Wholeness.

Again, this verse was not intended to communicate to us a continuing need for healing. It's intended to declare to the Israelites that they are healed and whole because they are no longer associated with Egypt. They've been redeemed!

For us, it is meant to communicate that we are healed and whole because we are no longer associated with sin—we are fully redeemed!

Just as no one was left in Egypt (sin), no one was left in sin. Jesus did a complete work. Your mind wasn't left in sin, and your body wasn't left in sin—every part of you was completely redeemed from sin: *spirit, soul, and body; your entire being.*

As Deuteronomy 7:15 pointed out, there was a 'have known' relationship between Israel and the diseases of Egypt. He said none, or not one of the diseases of Egypt which you have known will come on you. So, there had been a 'have known' relationship, or association. In other words, they had been familiar with the diseases of Egypt.

Do you have a 'have known' relationship with sickness, disease, or lack of any kind? If so, by the time you finish reading this book, I hope you'll recognize that your familiarity with sickness and disease should be a thing of the past —FINISHED!

God is saying, "You have known sickness and disease but because I AM *Yahweh Rapha* that relationship is now past tense — FINISHED! And you will have none of the diseases of Egypt. Why? —because I AM *Yahweh Rapha*! Because I AM in your midst."

In these verses, they're on the God side of the Red Sea, not on Pharaoh's side, enslaved in Egypt. And on God's side, there is an impassable sea of blood! We could say it this way: as certainly as Egypt is behind you, so is disease! Remember, Egypt was a type of sin.

For us, the message is: *As certainly as sin is behind you, so is disease!*

I'm not talking about behavior. We're talking about the condition of mankind after the fall, walking in a fallen mindset, a distorted sense of identity. Because whether we realize it or not, sin is behind us. For humanity born after the cross, sin never had anything to do with us because we weren't even born yet when He put away sin by the sacrifice of Himself. By the time we were born, sin had already been put away by Jesus two thousand years ago.

That term 'put away' means canceled. We weren't even born when sin was canceled, therefore, it has never had any relationship with us. And yet, we have been brought up in church to believe that we have a relationship with sin (aka sin nature or Adamic nature) until we "got saved," asking Jesus into our hearts, and started going to church.

But here's the point — as certainly as sin is behind us, so is sickness and disease.

This is what God is saying to them: "You have none of the diseases *of* Egypt because I AM Yahweh Rapha!" Or you could say it this way: if they were delivered from Pharaoh—and they were —and if they were beyond the boundaries of Egypt—and they were—then they were also beyond the territorial reach of sickness and disease!

Likewise, for us, we are beyond the reach of sickness and disease. We are free to walk entirely healed and whole all the time!

Chapter 6

Eternal Covenant of Wholeness

Exodus 14:30 says, "That day the LORD **saved** Israel from the hand of the Egyptians, **and Israel saw** the Egyptians dead on the shore." There are two things we need to see in this verse. First, they were saved that day from the hand of the Egyptians. Second, after being saved, they saw the Egyptians dead on the seashore. Moses had told them to stand still and see the salvation of the Lord. They saw the effects of their salvation. Their salvation was deliverance from their bondage to Egypt. They were saved, and they saw those who enslaved them, the Egyptians, dead on the seashore.

This happened to them but was written for us. It was written for our mind placement, for our mind's instruction. But sadly, we've failed to grasp what this story means for us because we've had a wrong understanding of the word 'saved' or *sozo*.

By watering down the meaning of the word and not understanding it's full meaning, we missed the amazing
FINISHED truth that death and all its attributes—sickness,
disease, lack, fear, and more—died on the cross and are no
longer in our midst.

We've often misunderstood the word 'saved,' reducing it to receiving
eternal life, avoiding hell, and having our sins forgiven. We've treated
it as something we must earn or obtain—by asking Jesus into our
hearts, repenting, getting baptized, stopping sinning, and so forth. But
'saved'—*sozo* in Greek and *yasha* in Hebrew—is a weighty word. It is a
word of complete freedom meaning to deliver, rescue, liberate, and
achieve victory. It signifies being made whole and complete, undamaged, unbroken, lacking nothing.

Being 'saved' also means a total transfer—from one realm, one reality,
and one experience to another entirely different realm, reality, and
experience. The Israelites experienced this firsthand. They were
saved, meaning they were completely delivered from the realm of
Egypt, the power of Pharaoh, and the harsh experiences of the Egyptians. They were utterly liberated and given victory over Pharaoh,
Egypt, and the Egyptians!

In Hebrew, it says, '...and saved *Yahweh* that day.' We often think this
refers only to that specific day for Israel. But in Hebrew, there's an
untranslatable word after 'that day.' It says, '...and saved *Yahweh* that
day *Aleph-Tav*.' *Aleph Tav* is a prophetic marker pointing to Jesus. In
Revelation, John describes Jesus as the *Alpha* and *Omega* in Greek.

The Hebrew equivalent is *Aleph Tav*. These two letters mean 'power' and 'cross' in Hebrew, or literally, 'the power of the cross.' Then it continues, '...from the hand of Egypt.' *Yahweh* (Jesus, I AM, the *Aleph Tav*) saved humanity from the hand or power of sin.

Israel was experiencing the FINISHED work of their *eternal* salvation on the day they were delivered or rescued from Egypt.

On that day, they were redeemed from Egypt and transferred from the reality and experience of being enslaved to Egypt onto the God side of the Red Sea.

But remember, it was written for our instruction—for our mind placement. So, what are we to understand from this part of the verse? First, that salvation had been eternally decided in the heavenly places (Exodus 14:30—the *Aleph Tav* points to the eternal covenant with man in Christ; see also 2 Timothy 1:9–10). The word 'saved' is not about praying a prayer and going to heaven someday and avoiding hell. It's the transfer from one realm, one reality, and one experience to another. It is being rescued and given liberty and victory over sin and death!

So, when were we saved? Salvation is not a one-time event. God saved us in Christ in eternity past. We were also saved two thousand years ago at the cross. We were saved when we woke up and believed what Jesus did. And we are being saved daily—or should be—by walking daily in the experience of our salvation: in health, prosperity, wholeness, and liberty in every area!

In 2 Timothy 1:9, it says, *"Who hath saved us, and called us with a holy calling, not according to our works, but according to his own purpose and grace, which was given us in Christ Jesus before the world began."*

Again, the Greek word 'saved' is *sozo*, and it means to live saved, live protected, live healthily, do well, and be whole.

And verse 10 says, *"But is now made manifest by the appearance of our Savior Jesus Christ, who hath abolished death and brought life and immortality to light through the gospel."*

Jesus appeared and made our salvation manifest—He made it clear, plain, and apparent. Strong's Concordance says that Jesus made our salvation graspable! He abolished death and enlightened us on what God-life (*zoe*) and immortality look like. He shed light on what had always been true about us—our salvation before the foundation of the world. He revealed that we were in God's plans safe, protected, healed, well, whole—saved—before God said, 'Let there be light!'"

We were sealed in Christ before the foundation of the world or before the fall!

And the second thing we are to see in this verse is *they saw the Egyptians dead* on the seashore. The word 'saw' means to perceive or to understand. Egypt was a type of sin, and the Egyptians were a type of death, including sickness, disease, lack, fear, and more—all of this and more died on the seashore (i.e., on the cross) 2,000 years ago. Jesus destroyed sin and death. He crushed sickness, disease, poverty, and anything else that caused us to live below the God-life we were designed to walk in. They were supposed to remain dead, but some have revived them. How? By becoming once again familiar with sickness and disease.

Remember, Deuteronomy 7:15 says, 'The diseases *of* Egypt which you have known.' 'Have known' is past tense. We weren't supposed to continue being familiar with sickness and disease.

But we haven't fully grasped that the fullness of our salvation includes seeing sickness and disease dead on the seashore—on the cross!

And so, we have co-existed with them, considering them normal. We have accepted cancer, heart disease, diabetes, and more as inevitable —just a part of aging, bad food choices, genetics, etc. But the truth is that the Lion of Judah roared, "IT IS FINISHED," overthrowing all sickness, disease, poverty, fear, lack, depression, addiction, and more! We haven't realized that God has already slain them for our benefit— He overthrew them in the midst of the sea.

The only connection with sickness and disease is sin—and sin was destroyed two thousand years ago.

We haven't understood that sickness and disease are not of biological origin. All diseases originated and sprung up from sin—Deuteronomy 7:15 says, "The terrible diseases *of* Egypt," (type of sin).

BUT Jesus put away the condition of sin by the sacrifice of Himself once for all. We haven't fully grasped that because He wholly crushed and destroyed sin—death and all that came with it, like sickness and disease, no longer exists—unless we remain sin conscious. Because where there is a consciousness of sin, there is a consciousness of death and all of its attributes. In 1 Corinthians 15:56 says that "The sting of death is sin." But apart from sin, death has no power, no existence.

Paul said in Romans 6:11, *"Reckon yourself dead to sin and alive to God!"*

Our thinking must change. We must see sickness and disease as they really are—dead on the seashore; dead on the cross and overthrown by Jesus. It's time to make up our minds to think differently and to agree with God. However, because we have been more familiar with sickness and disease than with the revelation of FINISHED, it might take time for that realm and that language to become familiar to us.

Abba doesn't want us to live from miracle to miracle, from healing to healing, but rather to live in the fruit that remains. To live in the revelation that because He is the health of our body—health is always the manifested experience in our life.

Let's go back to Exodus 15, verse 26 again. It says, "I will put none of the diseases upon you that I have brought upon the Egyptians for (*because*) I AM the Lord who heals you." This statement reminds me of John 10:10, "The thief comes not but to steal, kill and destroy, but I have come that you might have life and life more abundantly."

God, right here, is drawing a line of demarcation in these verses. He says none of the diseases *of* Egypt will be upon you. Why? He said, "Because I AM the Lord, your Healer"—or literally, because I AM the Lord, your Health, your Wholeness.

The word 'because' communicates a separation. He says we're no longer of sin and disease—because we're *of* Him, and He is our health, our wholeness. We are no longer associated with sin and disease because we're only associated or identified, with Christ.

He is our identity. He is wholeness, health, and abundant life in us. And as He is, so are we in this world! He is perfect health and well-being in every respect—in Him, there is no sickness, no disease, no lack—no death whatsoever. And we are one with Him, He is in us, and we are in Him.

> *Therefore, there is no sickness, no disease, no death whatsoever in us—only abundant life—His Resurrection Life!*

God wanted this to be absolutely 100% clear to Israel and to us. In verse 25, it says, "He made a statute and an ordinance for them. And this is the statute and ordinance: 'I'll put none of these diseases on you which I have brought on the Egyptians BECAUSE I AM THE LORD YOUR HEALTH!'"

The word 'statute' means to point or decree. And the word 'ordinance 'means a regulation or law. We're being told here that God decreed a regulation, a universal law, concerning the health and wholeness of His people. He decreed it.

For us, it's Romans 8:2, "For the law of the Spirit of life in Christ Jesus has made me free from the law of sin and death." And with the word death, we can include its attributes sickness, disease, poverty, fear, lack, etc.

Note: Again, don't get hung up in Exodus 15:25, where it sounds like God put the diseases on Egypt and He was the one who could put them on Israel. Remember, we're *only* pulling out the grace, glory, and good news of Jesus Christ from these Old Testament verses. All mankind before the cross walked in a distorted understanding of who they were and who God was—no one was exempt. Jesus said, 'No one knows the Father except Me.' They had a wrong interpretation of God.

The grace, glory, and good news of Jesus Christ is that He fully brought them out *of* Egypt, and He is their identity—He is their Health and Wholeness.

For us, the grace, glory, and good news of Jesus Christ is that He fully redeemed us from sin, and our identity is found in Him—we are whole in Him.

Exodus 23:25 says, "And ye shall serve the LORD your God, and He shall bless thy bread, and thy water; and will take sickness away from the midst of thee." This verse is a few months after Exodus 15. They have been completely redeemed from Egypt, and God has already declared to them that He is their Health.

Here in chapter 23, verse 25, He says, "I will take sickness away from the midst of thee." The phrase, "I will take away sickness" is in the perfect tense in Hebrew. It describes actions that have occurred in the past; completed actions (even if it is in the present or future tense) —it is a FINISHED tense! God is telling them what He has done and *will continue to do* in their lives.

In Hebrew, this verse literally says, "I turn aside sickness from within you, or from inside you." FINISHED! DONE! It wasn't confirming His promise but rather stating what He had already done—I HAVE TURNED aside sickness from within you.

And don't try to spiritualize this verse by limiting sickness to spiritual sickness.

The word 'sickness' here is *machaleh* and means sickness, disease, infirmity. The root is *challah,* meaning to be weak or sick, to be diseased, or grievous. God said "I have taken it away!"

So, what is He saying to us in this?

He is saying, *"By My presence in you I have taken away or removed sickness from within you."* FINISHED!

Romans 8:11 says, *"If the same spirit that raised Christ Jesus from the dead dwells in you, He will quicken (give life) to your mortal body."*

The beauty of grace is that we also have freedom of choice. And God's never going to violate our freedom of choice. If you choose to identify with sin, death, sickness, and disease, you're free to do that. He won't force you to walk in what He's done for you. He hates to see you down on your knees on the seashore, breathing life into those dead things like sickness and disease, but it's your choice.

How do we resuscitate dead things like sickness and disease? By saying and believing things like, 'Oh, I've had this disease in my family for 50 years,' or, 'This is hereditary,' or, 'It's flu season.' But the good news of the Gospel is that you don't have to live with sickness, disease, lack, or fear! It's all dead on the seashore and has been for 2,000 years

.

> In Deuteronomy 1:3, it says, *"And it came to pass in the fortieth year, in the eleventh month, on the first day of the month, that Moses spoke unto the children of Israel, according unto all that the LORD had given him in commandment unto them."*

Before we move on, I want you to see that this verse is from their 40th year in the wilderness. This is 40 years after God fully redeemed them from Egypt and told them, 'I AM THE LORD WHO HEALS YOU—I AM the One who has turned aside sickness and disease from within you.'"

How was sickness within them? Because they had been familiar with the diseases of Egypt. They had developed a mindset of sickness and

disease from their time enslaved in Egypt. Similarly, we have had a
mentality of sickness and disease caused by a lack of identity—seeing
ourselves through a fallen way of thinking, in a false, distorted identity instead of as fully redeemed beloved sons in the image and likeness of Abba with authority over all things.

> In Deuteronomy 7:6-9, it says, "For you are a people
> holy to the LORD your God. The LORD, your
> God, has chosen you to be a people for His prized
> possession, above all peoples on the face of the
> earth. [7] The LORD did not set His affection on
> you and choose you because you were more
> numerous than the other peoples, for you were the
> fewest of all peoples. [8] But because the LORD
> loved you and kept the oath He swore to your
> fathers, He brought you out with a mighty hand
> and redeemed you from the house of slavery, from
> the hand of Pharaoh king of Egypt [9] Know there-
> fore that the LORD your God is God, the faithful
> God who keeps His covenant of loving devotion
> for a thousand generations of those who love Him
> and keep His commandments."

It says God kept the oath. He's referring to the oath He swore to
Abraham. What was the oath? That the Israelites would come out of
Egypt after 430 years of bondage. And verse 12 says, 'If you listen to
these ordinances and keep them carefully, the LORD your God will
keep His covenant with loving devotion, as He swore to your fathers.'
Who are the fathers that He swore to? I believe He's talking about
what He swore to *their* fathers 40 years ago.

Verses 13-15 says, "*He will love you and bless you
and multiply you. He will bless the fruit of your
womb and the produce of your land — your grain,
new wine, and oil — the young of your herds, and
the newborn of your flocks, in the land that He
swore to your fathers to give you. ¹⁴ You will be
blessed above all peoples; among you, there will be
no barren man or woman or livestock ¹⁵ And the
LORD will remove from you all sickness. He will
not lay upon you any of the terrible diseases you
knew in Egypt,* ~~but He will inflict them on all who
hate you.~~*"*

Before we get into these verses, let's scratch out "He will inflict them
on all who hate you." This is not the nature of God that Jesus
revealed to us. So we will leave it in the Old Testament and not bring
it forward in our thinking.

So, in these verses, I believe He's referring to the oath He made with
the Israelites 40 years earlier, as well as the covenant He made with
Abraham, because He includes, 'I will remove from you all the
diseases of Egypt.' This was something God told the Israelites, not
Abraham, 40 years ago in Exodus 15:26.

Notice God says He will keep His covenant and mercy for a
thousand generations. Did you know it hasn't been a thousand generations yet? A generation is 40 years biblically. It hasn't been 40,000
years since the children of Israel came out of Egypt. Why is that
important? Because it shows us that a literal number isn't the point.

It's meant to convey that it's forever! He is telling them (and us), 'I'm keeping this covenant and mercy forever!'

The word translated 'mercy' here is *chesed* in Hebrew, meaning covenant love or loyalty to His covenant. But it's not loyalty in the sense that He must remain loyal to this covenant and mercy even if He doesn't want to. No!" *Chesed* is His covenant love for all humanity. It is His refusal to ever let us go!

He said the Lord will keep the covenant and kindness (*chesed*) which He swore to your fathers. In verses 13–15, we read what the covenant and kindness of God include—love, blessing, and abundance! And then again, He says, I have removed from you all sickness. FINISHED! The law of healing, divine health, and wholeness that He spoke to them in Exodus 23:25 is based on His covenant forever—His *eternal* covenant.

A final point in this verse is that two different words are used here—sickness and disease. We often use them interchangeably in Scripture, but they aren't. The word 'disease' is precisely how it sounds: 'DIS-ease.' It refers to weakness, pain, infirmity, or discomfort and is almost exclusively used concerning physical ailments.

The word 'sickness' is much broader. It means illness (or disease), anxiety, grief, calamity (or disasters). This word reaches into the soul, not just the physical body, and it also speaks to protection in every area of our life. All of this is His covenant of wholeness—His covenant of health, protection, provision, love, blessing, and abundance spoke here to Israel and to infinite generations—forever!

Our divine health and wholeness are an eternal reality given before the foundation of the world. Ezekiel 37:26 says, "Moreover I will make a covenant of peace with them; it shall be an everlasting covenant with them." This is not a future promise of making a covenant. It's past tense, FINISHED tense—God has made a covenant—an *eternal* covenant securing your health wholeness in Christ before time began. FINISHED!

Chapter 7

Health & Healing Is a Spiritual Law

W e are no longer under the law of sin and death, including sickness, disease, poverty, lack, fear, and more. I know I sound like I'm repeating myself, but like Paul, I don't find it tedious to repeat these truths to you. Continually reminding you of who you are and what He FINISHED in you gives you solid footing. It keeps you safe.

We are under the law of the spirit of life—health, prosperity, peace, joy, abundance, immortality—and are to expect to experience wholeness in every area of our lives!

In addition to being part of the covenant with God, healing and health are universal spiritual laws, just like gravity and electricity are universal natural laws. Because it's a universal spiritual law, we need to understand how to cooperate with it. Notice I said cooperate, not obey. Typically, in Christianity, we think of obedience to laws in the same way the Jews had to obey the Mosaic law or the Levitical law.

We are to understand the spiritual law of healing in the same way we understand the universal laws of nature. These laws operate irrespective of persons or circumstances, providing the same results for everyone all the time, regardless of who they are. For example, a murderer receives the same benefits of the law of gravity as I do. We all receive the same benefits from the laws of electricity and centrifugal force as well. These laws work together for the good of all humanity and the earth itself.

In Matthew 5:45, Jesus said that the Father makes His sun rise on the evil and the good and sends rain on the just and the unjust. This isn't just a statement about the goodness of God; Jesus was declaring a spiritual law. In other words, it never changes. He makes His sun rise on the good and the evil and sends His rain on the just and the unjust. It's a spiritual law and really has nothing to do with the goodness of God.

Of course, it does in a sense. But understanding it only as an action of God's goodness tends to link it in our thinking to our behavior and makes it seem conditional. By understanding it for what it truly is—a universal law—we see that it doesn't have anything to do with our behavior, actions, or circumstances. It is unchangeable and unconditional—the rain always falls, and the sun always rises no matter your circumstances, behaviors, or actions.

There are, of course, ways we can cooperate with spiritual laws to ensure we receive the greatest benefits. Conversely, there are ways we can put ourselves at risk by not cooperating with these laws, leading to harm. For instance, putting a fork in a toaster puts you in a dangerous situation with the laws of electricity. Or if you step off your 10th-story balcony because you don't believe in the law of gravity, you've placed yourself in an unsafe situation with it. Your unbelief in gravity doesn't change its effect. When you step off, the law of gravity will do the same thing for you as it would for me—it will draw us to the earth, causing us to fall and experience harm.

So, there are things we can do to put ourselves in an unsafe situation with these laws. However, there are also ways we can cooperate with them to derive the greatest benefits.

Now, it's crucial to understand that this chapter isn't about how to get healed. Our healing is part of the finished work that Jesus did. We just need our minds to awaken to that truth—we need a metanoia moment, an aha moment! We just need our thinking to shift.

Regarding the law of healing and health, we must understand that our relationship with the law of healing is affected only by two things—our belief and our expectation.

These are the only factors that can either conflict with or cooperate with the law of healing and health—what you believe and what you expect. And when I say belief, I'm not talking about us getting more faith for something. Belief is being persuaded about what His faith accomplished for us. So, in this chapter, I want to expand your expectations a little bit! I want to help you raise your level of expectation that all is FINISHED, so you can begin living a finished life, experiencing wholeness in every area.

Jesus has accomplished far more than what religion has given Him credit for. I don't believe we can ever think too big or believe too much that all is 100% FINISHED. We can never outthink God. While people might call it blasphemy or heresy, God doesn't. Our belief is being fully persuaded in what He knows to be true, in what His faith accomplished. I don't believe we've gone far enough in what we are to be persuaded about.

Let's look at another example in the story of the exodus.

> Exodus 15:25-26 says, *"Then he cried out to the LORD, and the LORD showed him a tree, and he threw it into the waters, and the waters became sweet. There He made for them a statute and regulation, and there He tested (proved) them. [26] And He said, 'If you will give earnest heed to the voice of the LORD your God, and do what is right in His sight, and give ear to His commandments, and keep all His statutes, I will put none of the diseases on you which I have put on the Egyptians; for I, the LORD, am your Healer.'"*

Hopefully, by now, you're beginning to see that the examples given to us in the Old Testament declare God's faithfulness to our enjoying a life of wholeness in all areas. These scriptures are not statements of obligatory requirements or commands that God has placed upon us to experience His favor and goodness. I know that's how many people read the Scriptures, both old and new covenants, as a 'do to get' or 'do to become.' But hopefully, by now, you're beginning to read them in this new light of FINISHED!

Understanding then that the scriptures are a declaration of God's faithfulness to our living a FINISHED life, I want you to see in Exodus 15:25–26 that *God became for them* this spiritual law of health and wholeness. Notice that He says in verse 25, "There He made for them a statute and regulation, and there He tested (or proved) them." What was the statute and ordinance? None of the diseases of Egypt *because I AM the Lord who heals you.*

The word LORD is Yahweh or I AM and refers to His *eternal* authority or dominion. He said *none* of the diseases of Egypt. Why? Because I AM the Authority who heals you. Because I AM the LORD that heals you.

What He's doing is becoming FOR them this law of
   healing and health.

He's saying I AM the Authority of health and
   healing.

All authority is rooted in law. For example, if there is no law like a 55 mile an hour speed limit, there can be no authority to enforce that law. In other words, it's not a law, and you can drive as fast as you want. So, God is giving His personality, His authority, to the law of healing and health and becoming the law of healing and health for them. In contrast, religion has looked at this and interpreted it in a dyslexic fashion.

He said, "If you diligently heed the voice of the Lord your God and do what is right in His sight, give ear to His commandments and keep all His statutes, I will put none of the diseases on you ~~which I have put on the Egyptians,~~ for I, the LORD, am your health."

So, when you read this, it should beg the question, didn't He also know that He would be the ONLY solution to the *"If you diligently heed the voice of the Lord your God and do what is right in His sight, give ear to His commandments and keep all His statutes?"*

In other words, didn't He know when He spoke this that He HIMSELF was the only solution? Didn't He know that there was no man on the face of the earth at the time that could fulfill these requirements? Of course, He knew! That was a function of this law — to satisfy that demand so that this law of healing and health might continue to be effective and efficient in people's lives producing healing and health.

So, knowing that, was He then giving us conditions required for healing? Because that's exactly what religion has done. That's what we've been taught. That healing is conditional on IF we do all that God requires. But God knew He was the only solution to this issue. He knew when He said this that Jesus was the ONLY solution to the "IF you ..." part of this passage. It was a function of the law of healing and health.

He wasn't giving us conditions that were required for our healing. But this is precisely where religious Christianity has become dyslexic down through the ages.

Notice it says at the bottom of the 25th verse, *"He tested them."* The KJV says *"He proved them."* In Hebrew, the word **proved** or **tested** is *nasah,* and means to test, try, prove, and by implication to attempt, adventure, and try. He was proving to them that their behavior was in no way associated with healing, just like they had nothing to do with the branch turning sweet. It's challenging to read Scriptures a certain way when you've been taught that it meant something else for generations. It makes it difficult for some to grasp that God was not providing us here with a list of behavioral requirements to be healed. He wasn't asking us to prove ourselves to Him! He wasn't testing our obedience! Or asking us to prove that we are faithful and obedient enough! No!

He was proving to them (and to us) that their behavior was in no way associated with healing. What He was doing was teaching them the spiritual law of healing and health. We're not talking about the Mosaic law—they didn't have that yet. They didn't receive that until chapter 20 in Exodus.

He's teaching them here the nature of spiritual laws. He's teaching the FINISHED work of His authority that was established from before time began.

The name I AM always communicates the eternal, not bound by time, nature of God. He was saying to them (and us), "It is BECAUSE I AM the Authority of your health and wholeness!" "BECAUSE I AM the LORD of your health and wholeness—*none* of the diseases of Egypt (a type of sin) will afflict you!"

We're not to interpret these Egyptians as a type of the world in contrast to the church, as in an "us and them" or "righteous and unrighteous" way of understanding them. Israel is a type of human-ity, and Judah in Israel is a type of church. But for years, we were taught that Israel was a type of the church, Judah a type of spirit-filled church, and everyone outside of the church is the world. Reli-gion has taught that because they are outside of the church, because they haven't repented of sin and asked Jesus into their hearts, they are not eligible for the benefits of these spiritual laws. This is absolute nonsense!

Israel represents the world—*all* mankind! So, the things spoken to Israel are written to indicate God's desire and His response to the world—to *all* humanity. God was in Christ reconciling the world. Knowing that He reconciled the entire world to Himself, when we go into the Old Testament types, it's impossible to see God reconciling only one small nation while everyone else is left to live a life separated from God.

We must learn to read the Old Testament through the lens of Christ, through the lens of FINISHED.

He's saying I AM the eternal Authority of your health and wholeness. I AM the eternal LORD of your health and wholeness. He's teaching them (and us) the spiritual law of the nature of healing and health and the fact that because it's a law, it has nothing to do with our behavior... good or evil. Just like gravity doesn't cease working for wrong behavior, everything just keeps working the way God ordained it to work. Because He is the eternal Authority, He is the eternal LORD who established ALL things... He is the Ruler who has placed ALL things into their operative functions.

Exodus 23:25 says, *"And you shall serve the LORD your God, and he shall bless your bread, and your water; and I will take sickness away from the midst of you."*

The Young's Literal Translation says, "*I have turned aside sickness from thine heart.*"

He wasn't speaking to Israel as a congregation, a church group, or a select chosen group of people, saying, "I'm going to take sickness out of the midst of the Israelites." He was referring to humanity — to ALL mankind — and He was saying I will take sickness out of the midst of you. He said I have turned aside sickness from within your heart. Notice that He is associating sickness with the heart rather than with the body. We don't do that. We usually associate sickness with the body. But this verse tells us that sickness originated in man's heart, not in the biology of man.

In biblical Hebraic understanding, the heart is the place where we feel feelings and think thoughts.

So, what does it mean to turn aside sickness from our heart? To me, this means addressing the root sickness in men's hearts—in their thoughts and feelings—that convinces them their *behavior* is linked to their wholeness or lack of health.

Remember, our cooperation with healing and health only involves two things—believing and expecting. Jesus said repeatedly be it unto you according to your faith. The word 'believe' is *pistis* in Greek and means to be persuaded. What are you persuaded of? What is your expectation? Be it unto you according to your expectations, according to your persuasions.

Sickness originated in the heart—in the thoughts and feelings of mankind. This concept was first introduced by the serpent to Adam. When God came looking for Adam, he hid because he was afraid and felt naked, or lacking. This fear and sense of lack showed how Adam's behavior was connected to his relationship with God in his mind. This sickness of the heart, affecting thoughts and feelings, made people believe that their actions determined their wholeness or lack thereof. This belief has been perpetuated in the church through the ages and still exists in the hearts of many believers today. We continue to believe that our wellness or lack of health is a result of our actions, whether good *or* bad.

Colossians 1:21 says, *"And you, that were some-times alienated and enemies in your mind by wicked works, yet now hath he reconciled."*

Notice the phrase *in your mind!* This isn't God's perspective of men —it was in their minds! They thought they were alienated from God. That's what Adam thought when he hid. What does it mean by wicked works? It says, by your wicked works or because of evil deeds. It doesn't mean that God turned away from them because of their wicked works! Instead, it means that because of their wicked works, they thought they were alienated from and enemies with God. All of us have experienced that!

We were taught that we were alienated from God because of "sin," by our wrong behavior, or our wicked works. But here in Colossians, we see that the root sickness in man's heart—in their thoughts and feelings—was the mindset that their behavior was somehow related to their experience with God, good or bad. Similarly, in Exodus with the Israelites, we see that they believed their good or bad behavior determined their wellness or lack of it.

Exodus 23:25 (Young's Literal Translation)
says, *"And ye have served Jehovah your God,*
and He hath blessed thy bread and thy water, and
I have turned aside sickness from thine heart."

This is reminiscent of Genesis 1:28, where God blessed them and said, "Be fruitful, multiply, fill the earth, and subdue it." The prophet Balaam affirmed, "What God has blessed, He cannot reverse." God cannot reverse what He has blessed. It's impossible! He said in Genesis 1:28, "I have blessed." That blessing is unconditional and unchanging.

In Exodus 23:25, He's simply reiterating His position from the beginning. It's not just since Egypt that He has blessed the bread and water and taken sickness away from their hearts — from their thoughts and feelings. God is saying to them, "Your behaviors have never affected My relationship with you or your wellness. From the very beginning, I have blessed your bread and water and turned away sickness from your hearts. It is the idea in your hearts that tells you your behaviors affect your access to healing and health—to experiencing and enjoying wholeness in every area of your life."

This is a powerful truth! He's communicating spiritual law. He's assuring us of absolute certainty. He's saying, "I AM the Authority; I AM the LORD! I AM the One who decided since before the foundation of the earth that your behaviors — what you do or don't do — have nothing to do with accessing health and wholeness. It's always been yours."

Mankind's health and wholeness were never conditional and never a someday truth to look forward to. It is an *eternal* truth, woven into the very fabric of our identity. We have always been whole and complete in Christ.

Part Two

Healed Is A Finished Work

Chapter 8

Jesus Healed Them ALL!

And all the multitude were seeking to touch Him, because power from Him was going forth, and He was healing all. — Luke 6:19 (*Young's Literal Translation*)

I am passionate about the subject of healing, divine health, and empowering people to live life experiencing the wholeness or fullness of their redemption. For this book, I chose a magnolia because it represents health and wholeness. I love that this one is a hand-drawn sketch of a magnolia. To me, that speaks of something personal, intimate, and one of a kind. This mirrors how Jesus, in the gospels, reveals Abba's desire to heal people. He shows us that not only does Abba desire to heal, but He also created us to be whole and complete in every area of our lives—spiritually, mentally, physically, financially, and socially.

Out of all the things Jesus did while here on earth, it seems He took particular delight in healing people and making them whole. Like this hand-drawn sketch of a magnolia, His healing ministry was personal and intimate, delighting in our one-of-a-kind uniqueness.

Six years ago, I read Luke 6:19, and the word "ALL" literally jumped off the page and came alive in my heart. My mind shifted, and I embraced the idea that God's will is to always heal ALL people.

My husband and I had started a gathering of people who, like us, had no church to go to anymore (which is a long story for another day and another book). I began teaching healing from the perspective that Jesus healed them ALL. As I taught that ALL were healed, people were set free from their wrong thinking about healing. Their misconceptions about God as their Healer began to fall away. Instead of seeing healing as an "if it be God's will" or a "maybe" from God, they began to understand that God's will is always to heal and that He never turns anyone away.

Luke always connects Jesus' healing ministry with His teaching. I think that's important. I found that when it comes to experiencing healing, people just need to be taught to think differently. They had been taught that maybe God heals, or sometimes He heals, which causes them to question whether He will heal *them*.

All they needed was to change their thinking and embrace the truth that healing is always God's will for ALL.

As a result, we started to see healings manifest as people embraced the word ALL. We saw cancer disappear, broken bones made whole, heart defects healed, people rising from wheelchairs, words spoken for the first time, and so much more! Such beautiful manifestations of healing simply from teaching and connecting the word ALL and ALWAYS to God's will for our healing! Once this truth unfolds in you, you can never go back to the way you used to think.

Luke 6:19 in the Mirror Bible is excellent! It says, "Everyone in the crowd was pressing in to touch Him because power was surging from Him, and He healed them all, one by one." I love this verse. Sometimes we read verses and don't pause long enough to allow them to create a picture in our minds. Jesus healed them ALL, one by one.

Can you see Him?

Walking through the crowds joyfully laughing, chatting with them, embracing them with passionate hugs—just loving on everyone, delighting in them! And delighting in tenderly healing each and every one of them. Can you see the intimacy, the passion, and the all-consuming love for each one of them?

We read stories like Jesus healing the man who was paralyzed at the pool of Bethesda and think that He only healed the one person while everyone else was left to remain sick. But I wonder about that. Scripture doesn't say everyone there that day was left sick, nor does it say they were all healed. This leaves us to imagine what that day looked like. Considering Luke 6:19, where we're told He healed them ALL, and Luke 5:17, where the power of God was present to heal (implying ALL that were there), it opens our minds to a broader picture.

The Mirror Bible says, *the very atmosphere was charged with the power to heal!*

Knowing that, can you really imagine that Jesus walked through and only healed one person lying by that pool? I can't. It would be like, as a mom, only cooking dinner for one of my kids. They're ALL hungry, but I choose to only feed one of them. Maybe because the others didn't spend time with me in the kitchen while I was cooking, or perhaps they didn't ask correctly or with "enough faith," or maybe it was to teach them a lesson. Do you see what I mean? That's ridiculous! I feed them ALL because I delight in them... *in each and every one of them.*

So, allow your understanding of God's nature as Love to ignite your imagination when you read the Bible. Ask Holy Spirit to show you what it looks like as if you were watching a movie. I promise you, it will be bigger, better, and much more inclusive of all people than you previously thought. It will always include ALL and reveal a FINISHED perspective!

I don't want to preach to you in this book about what I believe regarding healing. I want to simply examine Scripture through the lens of FINISHED. Let's put aside our preconceived ideas and beliefs on healing, along with our personal experiences, and just see what God says in His written word. More importantly, let's focus on what He says IN and BY His Word (the *Logos*: Jesus).

In this chapter, we're going to look at Jesus' ministry of healing—specifically, about Him healing ALL. I'll explain some of the meanings of the words in the verses related to healing so that you can see He is talking about physical healing. Sometimes we tend to spiritualize healing, thinking that God is more interested in the healing and well-being of our spirit rather than our physical bodies. But that's not true. Abba created your entire being (spirit, soul, and physical body) to be healed, whole, and complete. We can't look at all the verses because there are just too many, but I encourage you to do your own study.

> In Acts 10:38, it says, *"God anointed Jesus of Nazareth with the Holy Ghost and with power: who went about doing good and healing ALL that were oppressed of the devil; for God was with Him."*

The word 'healing' in this verse is *iaomai* and means supernatural healing, bringing attention to the Lord as our Healer. It also means to cure and restore health.

The word 'oppressed' is *katadunasteo* and means overpowered and dominated. It is to be brought down from the higher level of blessing that we should be enjoying in life.

The word 'devil' is *diabolo* and means slanderer or false accuser.

In other words, Jesus was anointed by God with the Spirit and the power to do good and heal ALL that were being ruled, overpowered, and dominated by the fallen mindset (*diabolos*). They were walking in the lie that they were not already God's image and likeness. And this fallen mindset, this false distorted Adamic identity, was affecting the health of their physical bodies and/or their mental health.

I love the phrase, "*... for God was with Him.*" He was co-participating with the Father and the Spirit. This tells us that healing was not just something Jesus did, but also the Father and the Spirit loved healing people and doing good! They were of one mind and heart in the matter of healing and doing good to ALL. God healed because He is Healer. He does good because He is Good. And anything we believed about the God of the Old Testament that doesn't align with that needs to change in our thinking. This verse shows Jesus revealing a God who loves healing and doing good to ALL!

Matthew 12:15 says, "*And great multitudes followed Him, and He healed them ALL.*"

The word 'healed' in this verse is *therapeuo*, meaning to heal and to cure. It is to reverse a physical condition and restore a person having an illness (disease, infirmity).

This same story is in Matthew 15:30. It says that "The great multitudes came unto Him, having with them those that were lame, blind, dumb, maimed, and many others and they were cast down at Jesus' feet, and He healed them."

Who was healed? Everyone that was brought to Him was healed. Who was brought to Him? The lame, blind, dumb, maimed, and many others. And ALL of them were healed. And verse 31 says that "The crowds marveled and glorified God!" Restoration of health, and our experiencing restored health and wholeness ALWAYS glorifies God!

Luke 6:19 says, "*And the whole multitude sought to touch Him: for there went virtue out of Him and He healed them ALL.*"

The word 'virtue' is *dunamis* and means miracle working power that is dynamic in its working.

The phrase 'out of' is two words, *ek,* meaning out from within and *erchomai,* meaning to come and go, and to bring and arrive.

The word 'healed' is *therapeuo,* meaning to heal and cure, and reverse a physical condition and restore health.

Dynamic miracle working healing power from within Him flowed out of Him and brought healing to ALL and restored them to wholeness. That same dynamic miracle working power is within us and flows out of to bring healing to all those we encounter.

In Matthew 14:14, it says, *"When He went ashore, He saw a large crowd, and felt compassion for them and healed their sick."*

It says He was moved with 'compassion' which is *splagchnizomai*. In other words, His heart was moved. He felt the deep emotions of sympathy and empathy.... *He had tender mercy on them.* I love that! This is what the response of mercy and compassion from Jesus looks like...*healing, restoring health, reversing a physical condition, curing diseases and illnesses, and making ALL people whole!*

Luke 4:40: *"Now when the sun was setting, all they that had any sick with divers diseases brought them unto Him; and He laid His hands on each one of them and healed them."*

The word 'ailing' is *astheno* meaning weak or feeble.

And 'disease' is *nosos,* which means an incurable chronic disease.

"In other words, those who had received devastating diagnoses and were given no chance of survival, left to suffer incurable diseases, were brought to Him. Those whose conditions had left them without hope, facing terminal prognoses. And it says that He healed each one of them—ALL! He laid His hands tenderly upon each one.

The commentary Robertson Word Pictures in the New Testament says, *"Healing one by one with the tender touch upon each one. Luke alone gives this graphic detail which was more than a mere ceremonial laying on of hands. Clearly the cures of Jesus reached the physical, mental, and spiritual planes of human nature. He is Lord of life and acted here as Master of each case as it came."*

I love this healing account. Luke just has such a way of painting a picture with His words. Can't you see it? Can you see the tender compassion of God in this verse?

It happened when the sun was setting. Why is that important? Because the Sabbath was over. They weren't allowed to carry the sick to Him until the end of the Sabbath. Religious traditions kept them from being healed, keeping them bound to sickness. This was not the Sabbath God had designed for them. God didn't create man for the Sabbath but rather the Sabbath was created for us.

And so, Jesus tenderly went to *each one* setting them free... *restoring them to their God-given health and wholeness.*

Luke 9:11 says, *"And the people, when they knew it, followed him: and He received them, and spoke unto them of the kingdom of God, and healed them that had need of healing."*

The phrase 'received them' is *apodechomai*, meaning He gladly welcomed, embraced, and heartily received them.

The word 'healing' in this verse is *therapeia,* and means care or attention, talking about the medical treatment received. It focuses on the reversal of physical illness or disease.

The word 'cured' is *iaomai,* and means supernatural healing. It is to restore health or wholeness.

The Mirror Bible says, "But it was not possible to hide from the massive crowd who kept following Him and receiving them kindly He continued to speak to them of the kingdom of God and curing whoever needed healing."

Again, I love the mental picture you get from Luke's words. The verbs in this verse are all imperfect verbs that suggest continued actions. The crowds **continued** to follow Him, and He **continued** to tell them about the kingdom of God, **continuing** to release super-natural healing restoring them to health and making them whole.

In Luke 17, we're told that the kingdom of God is within us. Jesus reveals to us what it looks like to live as a son made in Abba's image and likeness, created to rule, and reign in life. The kingdom of God is within us—the same healing power in Jesus is in us. And then He made tangibly visible what we as sons already possess by **continuing** to release supernatural healing restoring them to health and wholeness.

I'm undone reading these verses, realizing that crowds and crowds of people continually kept following Jesus, needing to be healed. Religion offered them nothing! Luke 5:17 says that "The power of God was present to heal." The Mirror Bible says, "The atmosphere was charged with the presence of the Lord to heal!"

The very atmosphere was charged with the healing power of God wherever Jesus went! Can you see it? Everywhere He went, there was healing power being released from Him. He lives in us! That means your entire body is charged with the presence of the Lord to heal! It is charged with resurrection life, the *zoe* life of God. The healing power of the One who restored your health and made you whole two thousand years ago *is inside you!*

Matthew 9:35 says, *"Jesus was going through all the cities and villages, teaching in their synagogues,*

and proclaiming the gospel of the kingdom, and
healing every disease and every sickness."

The word 'disease' is *nosos,* meaning a chronic, persisting disease, typically incurable.

The word 'sickness' is *malakia,* meaning a disease or condition that weakens you

The word 'every' is *pas* in Greek, meaning the whole, or ALL!

Jesus proclaimed the good news of the kingdom. **He healed every disease and every sickness He encountered—He healed ALL!** He restored everyone's health and wholeness completely.

Mark 3:10, *"For He had healed so many that the sick*
   kept pushing forward just so they could touch
   Jesus."

As a result of seeing Jesus heal everyone He encountered, the sick continued to press around Him and try to touch Him. The phrase 'pressed around' is *epipipto and* means to embrace with affection or seize with violence. In other words, they were falling upon him to such an extent that it was dangerous. They were not hostile but rather intensely eager.

It's an extraordinarily moving and overwhelming scene. Each one was embracing Jesus, falling upon Him, and persisting to get a personal touch from Him that would change their bodies and rid them of their illness.

> *This was not done in an orderly fashion like our*
> *healing lines at church. There were no ushers*
> *making sure everyone stayed in line and waited*
> *their turn.*

> *It was chaotic, messy, and, most of all, passionate.*

A great multitude had come from miles and miles away because they had heard about everything he was doing. This account is also in Luke 6, and in verse 18, it says that **they had come from all over, determined to hear Him teach and be healed of their diseases.** Their minds were made up, and they weren't going home sick. And Luke declares in verse 19, ***"And He healed them ALL, one by one!"***

Then He spoke these words (which are best translated in the Mirror Bible), "To be reduced to the most extreme state of poverty, does not define you. Disaster is not the fruit of fate or karma (performance-based religion)! The blessing of knowing, that the Kingdom of God belongs to you personally and that it is oozing from you, is the essence of your well-being and identity!" Wow! The kingdom of God oozes from us! It is the essence of our wholeness and identity, radiating from within us and transforming everyone we encounter!

Mark 7:37: They were utterly astonished, saying, *"He
   has done all things well; He makes even the deaf
   to hear and the mute to speak."*

Mark describes the people as utterly astonished at Jesus' remarkable
deeds, acknowledging, "He has done all things well; He makes even
the deaf to hear and the mute to speak."

This account is echoed in Matthew 15, where it's noted that the
people brought individuals with various afflictions—lame, crippled,
blind, mute, and many others—to Jesus, laying them at His feet. The
outcome was astounding: He healed them all.

Both Mark and Matthew portray the overwhelming response of the
crowds. Mark describes them as "overwhelmed beyond measure,"
while Matthew depicts them as "amazed" and glorifying God.

The Message Bible offers a vivid depiction of the scene:
*"When the people saw the mutes speaking, the maimed
healthy, the paraplegics walking around, the blind looking
around, they were astonished and let everyone know that **God
was blazingly alive among them**."*

I love that! What a visual—*God was blazingly alive among
them! Can you see it!?*

As I explored the verses recounting Jesus' healing ministry in the Gospels, I encountered countless instances of miraculous restoration. In fact, the overwhelming pattern reveals that ALL who sought healing from Him received it. It's a testament to the completeness of His work—a FINISHED reality where healing is not just possible but assured.

Yet, amidst this tide of miraculous interventions, I stumbled upon two exceptions—instances where the expected healing didn't manifest. However, even within these rare occurrences, the truth remains unshaken: healing is a finished work, accomplished for us and as us by the redemptive act of Christ.

Understanding this foundational truth, we recognize that while nothing can hinder our being healed, there are factors that can hinder our full experience of living life in a state of wholeness and restoration.

In Mark 6:5, it recounts an unusual occurrence during Jesus' ministry: "And He could do no miracle there except that He laid His hands on a few sick people and healed them."

This narrative is echoed in Matthew 13:54–58 and Luke 4:16–30. Mark specifically notes the limitation of miracles in that setting, highlighting that only a select few were healed. The term 'few' underscores the scarcity of healings—a stark departure from the usual abundance seen elsewhere in Jesus' ministry.

Matthew similarly remarks on the limited number of healings. Meanwhile, Luke, interestingly, omits mention of any healings altogether. Instead, he focuses on the skepticism and demands for miraculous signs that Jesus encountered as evidence of His claim of Messiahship.

They desired to witness the same signs and miracles that were occurring in Capernaum, yet in this instance, Jesus couldn't perform many miracles, and only a handful of sick individuals were healed.

Why? What hindered the flow of the miraculous? What led to the absence of the charged presence of the Lord for healing, as witnessed in Luke 5 just a short time later? Both Mark and Matthew attribute it to unbelief. Additionally, Mark mentions that they were offended by Him.

The term 'offended' originates from the Greek word "skandalizo," also used by Paul to describe the cross as a stumbling block. They were scandalized, but why? They viewed Him through merely human eyes—as Mary's son, a carpenter, a brother—blinded by unbelief and offense.

This veil of unbelief and offense led to explosive rage, even attempts to throw Him off a cliff. Some translations depict them stumbling at Him or turning against Him. Nothing hindered healing from God's side; rather, it was the blinding veil of unbelief and offense that obstructed their experience of God's healing power.

The other exception to healing ALL is found in Luke 5. The power of God was present to heal ALL in the room, yet only one person left healed: the paralyzed man lowered into the house through the roof by his friends. Luke vividly portrays the scene: they couldn't enter due to the crowded house, so they came through the roof. When Jesus saw him, His response was unexpected: "Your sins are forgiven!" But the man came seeking physical healing, not forgiveness of sins. Luke paints a vivid picture with his words, immersing us in the dramatic scene. Can you see it?

Jesus is teaching in the house, surrounded by people from all over, including Pharisees and Scholars of the Law. The atmosphere is charged with the presence of the Lord to heal (Mirror Bible). Suddenly, the roof tiles are removed, and a man is lowered through. Jesus effectively pulls the religious rug from under their feet, triggering controversy among the scribes and Pharisees. Whispering under their breath, they reason, "Who is this who speaks blasphemies? Who can forgive sin but God alone? Who does this man think he is!?" Jesus' words stirring controversy sparked confusion among them.

Jesus challenges them, "Which is easier to say: 'Your sins are forgiven' or 'Pick up your bed and walk'?" Then, He commands the man to rise, take up his bed, and go home. The people in the house are amazed, glorifying God, and filled with fear, exclaiming, "We have seen strange things here today." However, what was the 'strange thing' they witnessed? It couldn't have been the man getting healed; they were accustomed to seeing Jesus heal everyone He encountered, witnessing the miraculous wherever He went. The word 'strange' is *paradoxos* and means contrary to the opinion and contrary to expectation. Any of our opinions and expectations which are contrary to

God's opinions and expectations hinder our ability to experience healing. We're going to talk more about our expectations later in the book in the chapter on hope.

Let's dive into another powerful healing encounter found in Luke 5:12–13.before we end this chapter.

> Luke 5:12 – 13, it says, *"And it came to pass, when He was in a certain city, behold a man full of leprosy: who seeing Jesus fell on his face, and besought Him, saying, Lord, if thou wilt, thou canst make me clean. [13] And He put forth His hand, and touched him, saying, I will: be thou clean. And immediately, the leprosy departed from him."*

Here, we encounter a man afflicted with leprosy, a disease that rendered him ceremonially unclean and socially ostracized, living in a state of beggarly destitution. He was desperate—both Mark and Luke say he was begging Jesus. In fact, Mark says that he was on his knees begging Him. Despite his dire circumstances, when he saw Jesus, he approached Him and fell to his face, pleading, 'If you are willing, you are able to cleanse me.' The word 'able' implies a potent ability, enabled by dynamic miracle-working power in and through Jesus.

He didn't question Jesus' ability to heal him. He knew that Jesus was powerfully able! BUT his question reflects a common concern: is

Jesus willing to extend His healing touch to someone like *him*? F.F. Bruce said, "Men more easily believe in miraculous power than in miraculous love."

Leprosy was not only a physical ailment but also deemed highly contagious, leading to social ostracism. Lepers were mandated to ring a bell and cry out "unclean, unclean" to warn others of their presence, a practice steeped in degradation and humiliation. Beyond physical healing, the man longed to reclaim a life of dignity and freedom, embracing his identity as a cherished son of God. When he spotted Jesus passing by, he saw an opportunity for healing. However, there lingered a poignant question: would Jesus be willing to touch him, risking ceremonial uncleanness according to religious tradition?

Jesus' response is immediate! He reaches out and touches him. Then Jesus dealt with the man's heart (his thoughts and feelings) that questioned whether He was willing to heal him—He dealt with the man's IF regarding healing. Jesus' touch would physically heal this man, and His words would also heal his heart and mind. He says to him, *"I AM willing."*

"I love that the word we read as 'willing' in our English Bibles is in Greek capitalized, Thelo. He wasn't just willing to heal; Jesus is Willing. That's who He is. He is the Healer — He is Willing! As I was reading it, Holy Spirit highlighted that 'Willing' is not just an action Jesus does; it's who He is. He spoke to this man's heart (to his thoughts and feelings), saying, 'I AM Willing!' I AM *always* Willing to heal because 'Willing' is who I AM! And immediately, the leprosy left him

I AM is the eternal Name of God, and the attributes connected to the Name are eternal realities. In other words, God has always been Willing to heal because it's who He is. It has nothing to do with our behavior—good or bad. It's simply part of His eternal nature, not bound by time—He is always our Willing Healer!

In Ephesians 1:18, Paul prays for the enlightenment of our spiritual eyes, so we may grasp the depth of our inheritance in Christ, including the forgiveness of sins (verse 7). Healing and forgiveness are intertwined; they are inseparable components of God's redemptive work. Just as Jesus demonstrated his authority to forgive sins by healing the paralyzed man lowered through the roof, Ephesians 1:7 assures us of our forgiveness 'in Him.' Therefore, to experience healing is to experience the fullness of forgiveness, and vice versa. This truth underscores the FINISHED work of Christ—our healing and forgiveness are already accomplished in Him.

The same One who had the authority to forgive our sins also had the authority to heal our bodies! It's past tense, FINISHED truth — FORGIVEN AND HEALED! At the cross!

Why aren't we walking healed then? In Hosea 4:6a, it says, 'My people are destroyed for lack of knowledge.' Similarly, Isaiah 5:13a states, 'Therefore, my people go into captivity for lack of knowledge.'

The word 'captivity' is *galah* in Hebrew, meaning to denude in a disgraceful sense or stripped of its covering, possessions, or assets. It is to make bare.

That makes me think of Adam being naked and afraid. And God said to him, 'Who told you that you are naked?' God's response to Adam is the same response He gives us when we see ourselves lacking in health or wholeness. He says, 'Who told you that you were naked? Without My covering? Without my glory? Who told you that you were not whole, complete, and empowered with divine health? Who told you that you were enslaved to an enemy, and no longer image and likeness of Me with dominion over ALL things?'

Lack of knowledge of healing and wholeness as a FINISHED work destroys us. It causes us to be stripped of what is rightfully ours IN Christ—whole and complete, lacking nothing. How are we stripped of it? By not living life in the experience of who we are and what we have IN Christ."

Chapter 9

It Is Finished!

Lately, when I minister on healing, people often ask me about my personal experiences with healing. Their reason for asking is stems from the misconception that one's authority to minister on healing hinges on personal experiences of sickness and recovery. This notion is fundamentally flawed. The essence of Jesus' FINISHED work grants us abundant life—a life characterized by health and wholeness in every aspect. He has already eradicated sickness and disease from our lives. Therefore, my individual encounters with healing are inconsequential.

The only experience that holds weight is His sacrifice on the cross, where He conquered sickness and disease, co-resurrecting us with Him, whole and complete IN Him—fully alive with His resurrection life

Some seek personal testimonies for encouragement in their own healing journeys. However, in my experience, personal testimonies don't always have the desired effect. Each healing story is unique, and what resonates with one person may not necessarily resonate with another. This discrepancy can lead to dismissal if the healing seems too minor, or to feelings of discouragement and questioning if someone else receives healing while they don't.

The four Gospels are rich with personal testimonies of healing. If these accounts haven't convinced you that healing is always God's will and an integral part of the abundant life He offers, then my personal testimony may not sway you either.

However, personal testimonies can still ignite profound discussions. I've witnessed powerful conversations emerge when sharing stories of miracles with friends. Additionally, I've attended miracle healing services where remarkable healings occurred—deaf ears opened, broken bones mended, and cancers vanished, among other miracles. Yet, while these testimonies are impactful, our belief in healing must ultimately be grounded in the certainty of Christ's finished work.

In Luke 11:29, Jesus remarks on the growing crowds seeking signs. They clamored for more miracles, intoxicated in their unbelief, and addicted to the tangible. The Mirror Bible says they were intoxicated in their unbelief and addicted to the soul realm. Despite their thirst for signs, Jesus rebukes this generation, declaring that only the sign of Jonah will be given.

Jesus tells them, "If you fail to understand the symbolic, prophetic significance of Jonah, another sign is not going to make any difference" (Mirror Bible). The prophetic significance of Jonah was Jesus Christ being raised in three days and ALL of humanity raising with Him.

No matter how many testimonies, signs, wonders, or miracles we see and hear about, we won't live continually in the experience of being whole and complete in every area of life until we understand that our healing, our restored health is a FINISHED work.

So, I want to lay a foundation for our wholeness by looking at Jesus' final words: "IT IS FINISHED." God's abundant life for us, this FINISHED life, is not about continually seeking healing but about knowing that we have already been made whole. FINISHED! Completed two thousand years ago!

However, Abba will always meet us where we are. If healing is needed, He will meet you there. If comfort is necessary because of grief, He will meet you there. If courage is needed, He will meet you there. Even if you feel as if you are walking through the valley of the shadow of death and unable to see that death has no dominion over you, Abba will meet you there.

And in each of these places, Abba lovingly says, "Come up higher. See life from where you are seated, FAR ABOVE! Awake to who you are IN Christ, co-seated in heavenly places."

We are transformed by the renewing of our minds. That's not our job; it's something Holy Spirit has done. Titus 3:5 says, "He saved us, not by the righteous deeds we had done, but according to His mercy, through the washing of new birth and renewal by the Holy Spirit." He has saved us—spirit, soul, and body. The renewal of our minds by the Holy Spirit occurred two thousand years ago. Importantly, the word renewal isn't a verb; it's a noun. It's the renewal of our minds.

The word **renewal** is *anakainosis* in Greek which is from two words: *ana*, meaning upward, and *kainos*, meaning unprecedented, unheard of, unused, unworn, uncommon, different from anything previously seen, heard, or known.

It's the new mind, the *kainos mind* from above. It is the mind of Christ.

Romans 12:2 in the Passion Translation says, "Be inwardly transformed by the Holy Spirit through a total reformation of how you think." And 1 Corinthian 2:16 says, "We have the mind of Christ." The Amplified version of 1 Corinthians 2:16 says that "We hold His thoughts, His feelings, the intents, and the purposes of His heart."

We're not becoming more like Christ. We are already like Him.

John says in 1 John 4:17, "As He is, so are we in this world." Abba is simply waking us up to who we already are IN Christ. In Galatians 1:16, Paul says, "It pleased the Father to reveal His Son in me." Abba took great delight in awakening Paul to who he already was IN Christ. Psalm 17:15 declares, "As for me, I will see Your face in righteousness; I shall be satisfied when I awake in Your likeness." The Young's Literal Translation says, "I — in righteousness, I see Thy face; I am satisfied, in awaking, with Thy form!"

> It's time to wake up and know that we are sons made in the image and likeness of Abba!

> Our *kainos mind*, the mind of Christ, already knows divine health and wholeness is a FINISHED work in us.

In John 19:30, Jesus said, "IT IS FINISHED" and then died — ALL mankind and ALL that Adam had introduced into the world (sin and death) co-died with Him. The old man and everything that hindered mankind from living an abundant life died with Jesus that day. The word "FINISHED" is *tetelestai* in Greek, meaning ended, fulfilled, accomplished, completed, and perfected. It means to bring to a close. It communicates the consummation of ALL things; the conclusion of everything.

It is in the perfect passive tense, denoting an action completed in the past with effects continuing into the present and without end. Francois du Toit, author of the Mirror Bible, writes about this word: "The only possible way we can delay the glory that follows the cross is by underestimating what happened there when Jesus died and cried: 'It is finished!" What Jesus was saying was, "It is FINISHED! And the results of ALL being FINISHED will continue fully in your lives!"

ALL has been completed, is now complete, and will forever remain completed. IT IS FINISHED!

The work of man's redemption and salvation was completed, and the benefits of our redemption and salvation would continue in our lives! It was a full, complete redemption and a full, complete salvation (*sozo* – wholeness). Nothing was lacking in His FINISHED work. ALL was completed! FINISHED! Nothing else was needed or required from us or God. "FINISHED" indicates a position, a condition, a state of being, a resting place.

The word "FINISHED" was an accounting term used to mark a debt paid in full, and it was also a term used to show that a slave was no longer in bondage. As an artist term, it was declared when the artist stood back and announced, "The picture is perfect," and laid down his brush.

But my favorite meaning of the word is as a military term. It was shouted as the full and final victory over the enemy. It declared that the war or the battle was over. It was a call to lay down your weapons and go home. It was the signal of peace!

In John 17:4, Jesus said, "I have glorified thee on the earth: I have FINISHED the work which You gave Me to do." He FINISHED the work Abba gave Him to do. What was the work that He FINISHED? Adam's work! Jesus came to finish Adam's work so that you and I would have nothing to do except rest in what was FINISHED before time began. He was the Last Adam. When He said, "IT IS FINISHED," He made the first Adam (i.e., the old man) and all that the first Adam introduced into the world obsolete.

There isn't any residue of Adam in anyone—not in
     the believer and not in the pre-believer. None of
     Adam survived the cross.

IT IS FINISHED—ALL has been perfected,
     completed, and made whole.

Mark 15:37 says that Jesus uttered a loud cry and breathed His last. Luke 23:46 records, "Then Jesus, calling out with a loud voice, said, 'Father, into Your hands, I commit My Spirit!' And having said this, He breathed His last." What was the loud cry that Jesus cried out? IT IS FINISHED!

The word 'cry' is *phóné*, meaning a sound or a noise. Its root is *phemi*, meaning to bring to light. Light is revelation. When we make "IT IS FINISHED" our loud cry, we bring to light His completed work— releasing within us the revelation of who we are IN Christ—of who He is in us, and what He FINISHED for us and as us.

The word 'loud' is *megas*, meaning abundant, fierce, massive, more important, strong, too much, very much, much more!

Make your cry of "IT IS FINISHED" loud in your life! Make it fierce and overwhelming! Make it much more and greater than anything else! Release the revelation of your identity in Christ!

On the battlefield of sin and death that enslaved men and caused them to walk in a false, distorted identity, Jesus released the loud cry for us to lay our weapons down because the battle was FINISHED. It was a complete and final victory over the enemy! We don't have to battle for what is ours in Christ. We don't have to fight to get it, and we don't have to fight to keep or maintain it.

No spiritual warfare is necessary. There is no enemy to fight when the battle is FINISHED, and the enemy is defeated. There is no need to be on guard, keeping your weapons close at hand just in case the enemy comes back. Why? Because Jesus did a COMPLETE work—there is no "just in case" and never will be.

Colossians 2:15 says, *"Having disarmed the rulers and the authorities, He made a show of them in public, having triumphed over them in it."*

The word 'disarmed' is *apekdyomai* in Greek, meaning completely stripped! In Matthew 28:18, Jesus said, "ALL authority (ALL power) in heaven and on earth has been given to Me." He is Omnipotent— He is the ALL Power. There is no other power because ALL authority belongs to Jesus. There is only one power. There is no smaller or lesser power out to attack you or do battle with you.

IT IS FINISHED! You can safely lay your weapons down forever and simply rest in His FINISHED work.

But just how finished is FINISHED? How far does it reach, and what does it cover? We're going to explore that in the upcoming chapters of part two. We'll examine how He has made you completely whole and lacking nothing.

I see too many believers who are sick and dying needlessly. Healing lines at church are full of believers struggling with sickness. Pastors and well-meaning people often tell us we need more faith to get healed. But could the reason be what we believe, rather than how strong our faith is? Could it be because we believe we need to have enough faith to get healed or that we need to believe better?

In reality, we just haven't understood that believing is simply being persuaded of what He believes—in what His faith accomplished for us, and as us.

Maybe we haven't gone far enough in believing IT IS FINISHED.

What should our FINISHED life, or this new life IN Christ, look like? Paul showed us in Galatians 2:20 what his new FINISHED life looked like. His life in the flesh, in his physical body, was lived in the awareness of Christ IN him. Paul lived a life that was completely free of any association with Adam and the fall. A life free of any identification with sin and death. Free from ALL the effects of the fall—sickness, disease, poverty, fear, addiction, etc. He lived a life of zero sin consciousness.

Hebrews 10:2 tells us that the worshippers, once purified, should have no more consciousness of sins. This consciousness of sins refers specifically to the belief in a present and persistent fallen condition of man that continues to tell us that God is a rewarder or punisher, implying that our healing is determined by our behavior—good or bad.

Sin-consciousness is the New Testament equivalent of the tree of the knowledge of good and evil. It is our only tie to sickness and disease.

But the good news of the Gospel is that sickness and disease, sin and death, and ALL effects of the fall are null and void from God's perspective—defeated at the cross. FINISHED! If that is not also our perspective, then we won't see ourselves as dead to sin, dead to sickness and disease, dead to poverty and lack, dead to fear, and dead to death! We will not understand that we are alive only to God. We won't grasp that it is His life in us, and ALL the effects of sin and death are not part of our FINISHED life IN Christ.

This understanding of having no more consciousness of sin because we have been purified, because He has taken away the sin of the world, must be our foundation as we move forward in realizing that we are not just healed but whole in every area of our lives.

We need a correct understanding of the origin of sin in Genesis. Sin was not the action of eating from a forbidden tree; it wasn't behavior! Sin was believing the original lie that led to eating from the tree. God had made Adam and Eve whole, in His image and likeness, with all dominion, lacking nothing. Sin or transgression was their belief that they were not whole, that they weren't already like God, that they lacked something of Him. The result of that sin was the behavior that followed—eating from the tree of the knowledge of good and evil.

God says we are clean, pure, guiltless, upright, innocent, unstained, sinless. This is humanities identity in Christ right now, not when we pray the prayer or get to heaven someday. We are whole and lacking nothing!

What we believe about IT IS FINISHED determines our experience of the FINISHED life we
live in this world.

In Genesis 3:11, God said to Adam, *"Who told you that you were naked?"* In other words, who told you that you weren't whole, that you were lacking something? In truth, Adam and Eve weren't lacking anything. They were made in the image and likeness of God. But they believed the lie and consequently started living a life rooted in that lie. Having a false perception of themselves, God, and their world—living under the dominion of their five senses rather than in the awareness of their identity as beloved sons, destined to reign in life.

Sin in both Hebrew and Greek means to miss the mark, lose yourself, and wander from the way. It is to live below the life God intended for you.

What is the mark?

It is living an abundant life as sons made in His image
        and likeness. It is ruling and reigning as lords in
        this FINISHED life IN Christ.

Chapter 10

The Main Point part one

Now it happened, on a certain day, that He got into a boat with His disciples. And He said to them, 'Let us cross over to the other side of the lake.' And they launched out. ²³ But as they sailed, He fell asleep. And a windstorm came down on the lake, and they were filling with water, and were in jeopardy. ²⁴ And they came to Him and awoke Him, saying, 'Master, Master, we are perishing!' Then He arose and rebuked the wind and the raging of the water. And they ceased, and there was a calm. ²⁵ But He said to them, 'Where is your faith?' And they were afraid, and marveled, saying to one another, 'Who can this be? For He commands even the winds and water, and they obey Him!'"
— Luke 8:22 – 25

Jesus said, *"Let's go to the other side."* Sometimes in life, circumstances happen as in verse 22... a violent storm came while they were going across to the other side, filling up the boat.

The disciples are afraid they will die, but Jesus has already said,
"Let's pass over to the other side!"

During this storm, what was Jesus doing? He was asleep on a pillow.
He said, *"Let's pass over to the other side"* and then He fell asleep and
continued to sleep while a major windstorm came, and the waves
beat against the ship, filling it with water! But Jesus was undisturbed
during the storm! He wasn't just resting in His eyes—He was sound
asleep! At rest! What were the disciples doing? They were fearful,
panicking, and thinking they would perish or be destroyed.

But Jesus had already said, *"Let's pass over to the other side!"*

The verb 'let's pass over' is an aorist subjunctive tense. Meaning a
definite outcome will happen as a result of another stated action.
What was the other stated action? Jesus said, *"Let's pass over to the
other side."* His words declared the definite outcome. In Jesus' mind,
it was FINISHED!

But the disciples were looking at the circumstances before them.

The circumstances seemed dire, threatening to prevent them from
reaching the other side. In a state of panic, they woke Jesus, exclaiming, "Master, Master, we are perishing!" They were essentially pleading, "Doesn't it concern you that we're on the brink of disaster? Don't
you care that we're about to lose everything? Can't you see that we're
facing imminent death?"

In verse 24, Jesus rebuked the wind and commanded the sea to be calm and silent. The Mirror Bible notes that Jesus stood up with authority, not reacting with shock to the violent storm. Instantly, the wind ceased, and an extraordinary calm settled over the waters.

Interestingly, the root word for 'calm' in this verse is *gelao*; it means to laugh and smile as a sign of joy or satisfaction.

As I read the meaning of that word, I wondered if it referred to the wind and waves or the disciples! I pictured the disciples breathing a sigh of relief and laughing with joy!

Then Jesus turned to His disciples and asked, "Why do you have no faith?" He was challenging them to trust in the certainty of His words, "Let's go to the other side!"

Why weren't they fully persuaded that Jesus' words had the power to bring about the promised outcome? Why didn't they grasp that His declaration meant their safe arrival on the other side was already a FINISHED reality?

What about you? Do you trust in the certainty of His words? Do you believe that His promises are already a FINISHED reality in your life? Are there areas where you might still be looking at the storm instead of resting in His assurance?

As a Son, Jesus knew His Father always leads His sons in triumph (2 Corinthians 2:14). Not some of the time, but ALL the time—ALWAYS! And He doesn't cause us to barely get through. NO! He causes us to always triumph! Webster defines triumph as a great victory! We are always victorious! It's who we are. It's our identity. And the thesaurus lists as antonyms of triumph: disaster, failure, forfeit, loss, sadness, sorrow, unhappiness! It may look like a sudden storm of tragedy, failure, loss, or sorrow has hit your life, but Abba leads you in victory ALWAYS! Because in Christ, you've already crossed over to the other side.

We have the *kainos* mind, the mind of Christ—we hold the thoughts, the intents, and purposes of His heart. Our mindset or thinking needs to be the same as His when distracting circumstances try to throw us off course. We need to be in a position of rest, resting in IT IS FINISHED. Speaking with authority to those circumstances to be silent, knowing that our Daddy ALWAYS causes us to triumph because in Christ our triumph is a FINISHED work! That's ruling and reigning in life. Your understanding of IT IS FINISHED should be continually increasing and expanding.

It has been FINISHED—is right now FINISHED—and will forever remain FINISHED! It is always FINISHED because Jesus did a complete and complete and perfect work.

In this book, we're examining the healing ministry of Jesus as it pertains to us as a FINISHED work in the New Covenant; as our inheritance as new creations in Christ. Most of us have been exposed to the healing ministry of Jesus through the gospels, where He is the Healer continually healing ALL people.

But we live in the New Covenant. The Gospels reveal the Old Covenant relationship between God and man. The point of looking at the Gospel accounts of Jesus' healing in chapter eight was to secure in your thinking that God's will is always to heal. It is always about our restored health and wholeness.

From the New Covenant perspective, we see what Jesus did in His death and resurrection brought wholeness to every aspect of our lives. His goal was not for us to live life from healing to healing, but to recognize our FINISHED and COMPLETE wholeness and live in divine health.

Our wholeness and divine health are a FINISHED part of our redemption because we were made whole in our entire being (spirit, soul, and body). So, stick with me... we're going to look at a lot of verses in the coming chapters. Your revelation of FINISHED will increase even more as you begin seeing yourself as you truly are— whole and complete with nothing missing and nothing broken.

Hebrews 1:1–3 says, *"On many past occasions and in many different ways, God spoke to our fathers through the prophets. ² But in these last days, He*

has spoken to us by His Son, whom He appointed
heir of ALL things, and through whom He made
the universe. ³ The Son is the radiance of God's
glory and the exact representation of His nature,
upholding ALL things by His powerful word.
After He had provided purification for sins, He sat
down at the right hand of the Majesty on high."

Verse 2 says, "In these last days, God has spoken to us by His Son." The word "by" is not a bad translation here, but the actual Greek word is "en," which means "in." God has indeed spoken to us by His Son, but the word "en" is a position of rest! I love that!

What is communicated to us in and by the Son is a
FINISHED rest!

I like to use both words in this verse—"in" and "by"! This verse tells us that God said something to the world, to all mankind, in His Son, and by His Son. This isn't referring to the words Jesus spoke in red in our Bibles. It is referring to what God said through Jesus in His ministry to all humanity. It is what He spoke regarding our wholeness, our completeness, in and by Jesus.

And many haven't truly heard what God has spoken in and by His Son. When we talk about hearing something, we're not just talking about the words resonating in our ears. We're talking about hearing with understanding. Many have not yet heard and understood what is being referred to here, in these verses.

What God has spoken in and by His Son needs to be heard on the inside.

It needs to be a revelation in our hearts—in our thoughts and feelings.

Notice verse 3 says, "When He had by Himself purged our sins, He sat down at the right hand of the Majesty on high." This message is for all humanity. You would expect believers to understand and agree with this. Yet, many believers have not fully grasped the critical significance of these words: "He sat down."

We haven't fully understood the value and the immediate, right-now application of these words: "When He had by Himself purged our sins, He sat down at the right hand of the Majesty on high."

The word 'by' is *dia* in Greek, meaning entirely successfully through! Jesus completely and successfully purged sin with no help from us! The word 'at' is *en*, meaning in, and it denotes a position of rest. So... "He, by Himself (with no help from us), purged our sins (referring to ALL mankind's sins)." Then He sat down in rest at the right hand of the Majesty on High!

The writer of Hebrews says this is the main point of everything he's saying. He says, we have such a High Priest who is seated. The KJV uses the word *sum*: "it is the sum of everything He is saying." The word 'sum' means the total or the finality.

So, in other words, "He is seated" is the main point, the finality of what God has spoken in and by His Son.

Most think the cross was the main point. But His death on the cross was not the finality of all that the Father was speaking *in* and *by* His Son.

This doesn't mean that we should stop being thankful for the cross and the blood of Jesus. I'm not in any way trying to demean the value and power of the cross. But it's not the main point! It's not the finality of ALL the Father was speaking! It was necessary. It was something He had to do to arrive at the main point. But it wasn't the main point! As New Testament believers, we ought to at the very least begin with His resurrection—but even that is not the main point. The main point is "He is seated" and we are co-seated with Him.

Psalm 110:1 *"The LORD said to my Lord, 'Sit at My right hand, Till I make Your enemies Your footstool.'"*

This is the first occurrence in Scripture where we read about the Lord being seated. We also read about it in the gospels.

- Matthew 22:44 says, "*The Lord said to my lord, 'sit at my right hand till I make your enemies my footstool.'*"
- Mark 12:36 says, "*David himself said in the Holy Spirit, 'The Lord said to my Lord, "Sit at my right hand, until I make your enemies the footstool of your feet."'*"
- And in Luke 20:42–43, Jesus said, "*For David, himself says in the book of Psalms: 'Said the Lord to the Lord of me, sit at the right hand of Me, [43] until I place the enemies of You as a footstool at the feet of You.'*"
- Acts 2:32–35 says, "*This Jesus God raised up, and of that we all are witnesses. [33] Being therefore exalted at the right hand of God and having received from the Father the promise of the Holy Spirit, he has poured out this that you yourselves are seeing and hearing. [34] For David did not ascend into the heavens, but he himself says, 'The Lord said to my Lord, "Sit at my right hand, [35] until I make your enemies your footstool."'*"
- And Hebrews 1:13 says, "*But to which of the angels said He at any time, 'sit at my right hand, until I make thine enemies thy footstool?'*"

Why does this one statement warrant so much repetition in Scripture? It suggests that there is great importance in understanding the main point or the finality of everything being said.

What is the main point or finality of what God has spoken about our redemption? Our High Priest SAT DOWN!

The writer of Hebrews is saying this is what all of us need to hear and understand. We've all "heard" these verses at some point in our Christianity. But we haven't genuinely heard with understanding what they meant for us. This is the main point, the finality that God has spoken to us IN His Son to ALL the world. ALL mankind has a High Priest. This message is for the churched and unchurched, believers and pre-believers — it's talking to the world, ALL mankind!

The main point or finality of the revelation of our redemption is that we ALL have a High Priest who SAT DOWN.

> Hebrews 12:1–2 says, *"Therefore, since we also are surrounded by such a great cloud of witnesses, let us throw off everything that hinders and the sin that so easily entangles. And let us run with perseverance the race marked out for us, ² fixing our eyes on Jesus, the pioneer and perfecter of faith. For the joy set before Him, He endured the cross, scorning its shame, and SAT DOWN at the right hand of the throne of God."*

Hebrews 1:3 tells us that He purged our sins and SAT DOWN, and Hebrews 12:2 tells us that He endured the cross and SAT DOWN. Mark 16:19 says, "Therefore, the Lord Jesus, after speaking to them, was taken up into heaven and SAT DOWN at the right hand of God."

I believe there is something we're supposed to hear in this that we haven't yet heard. Something we're supposed to know deep down inside us, that we haven't understood. Something that will affect our life and allow us to fully experience ALL that He FINISHED.

So, what do we need to understand about His being seated?

> Revelation 3:21: *"To he who overcomes I will give to him to sit with Me on My throne as I also overcame and sat down with My Father in His throne."*

> Mirror Bible: [Through this door of my death as your death, and my resurrection as your resurrection] - *we now dine together in the throne room, celebrating your victory mirrored in mine! This is my gift to you; it is on exactly the same basis of my victory celebration and my joint seatedness with my Father in his throne-room!*

Notice what it says about Jesus, "... as I also overcame and sat down with My Father on His throne." So, the first thing we need to hear and understand is that Jesus SAT DOWN because He overcame. Remember Hebrews 1:3, which says, He purged ALL sin for ALL time for ALL people, and He sat down! In other words:

- He disarmed principalities, and powers and rulers—**and He sat down!**
- He destroyed death—**and He sat down!**
- He released those who were subject all their lives to bondage through the fear of death—**and He sat down!**
- He destroyed ALL the works of the devil—**and He sat down!**
- He bore our sicknesses and carried our diseases so that we would never have to—**and He sat down!**
- The chastisement for our peace was upon Him—**and He sat down!**
- He restored innocence and righteousness to ALL men —**and He sat down!**
- He restored and brought ALL sons face to face with Abba —**and He sat down!**

We could go on and on. But the point is that He's seated because everything that needed to be done is done. He FINISHED ALL, He overcame ALL—**and He SAT DOWN!**

There is nothing left for you and me to do because we're co-seated with Him. There is nothing left for religion to accomplish. There is nothing left for us to achieve. And there is nothing left for God to do! It's all perfected, completed, done! IT IS FINISHED!

Galatians 4:19 says, *"My little children, for whom I labor in birth again until Christ is formed in you."*

The Mirror Bible: *"... I travail for the full realization of Christ to be formed within you."*

We should be living victorious, whole, prosperous, and abundant lives. Yet, many today are living lives powerless to their circumstances—sick, broke, fearful, and in bondage to things like depression, addiction, sin, striving, and toiling.

Paul was passionate that the Galatians fully realize who they were in Christ and live their lives in the fullness of His life in them.

- Galatians 5:1 says, "It was for freedom that Christ set us free."
- 2 Corinthians 2:14 says, "He always causes us to triumph IN Christ Jesus."
- Romans 5:17 says, "How much more will those who receive the abundance of grace and the gift of righteousness reign in life through the One Man, Jesus Christ."
- 2 Peter 1:3 says, "He has given us ALL things that pertain to life and godliness."
- Hebrews 2:7–8, talking about mankind, says, "You made him a little lower than the angels (in Hebrew Elohim – God); You crowned him with glory and honor and placed everything under his feet."

We are free, we always triumph, and we rule and reign in this life. We have been given all things that pertain to life and godliness. We have been crowned with glory and honor and have all authority in this life. All of this stems from our position of being co-seated with

Him in the heavenlies—a position of rest. Jesus declared in John 19:30 and in Revelation 21:6–8, "IT IS FINISHED!"

From the Father's perspective, the fall never happened. This is a crucial truth we must grasp. Religion often perpetuates the fall in its teachings, impacting not only those within the church but also the wider world. However, Abba sees it differently because Jesus, the last Adam, completely fulfilled all of Adam's obedience.

God sees IN Christ a complete and total reversal of the fall and ALL its effects!

It is such a complete and total reversal that, as far as Abba is concerned, it's as if the fall never occurred. Therefore, since we strive to see things from Abba's perspective, this must also be our understanding. We need to recognize that in Christ, there was a complete and total reversal of the fall and that the reason He sat down is because ALL IS FINISHED.

The Father's perspective on the human condition under this New Covenant is perfectly summarized in Hebrews 8:12: "For I will forgive their iniquities and will remember their sins no more." The Mirror Bible further illuminates this by saying, "This knowledge of me will never again be based on sin-consciousness. My act of mercy, extended in Christ as the new Covenant, has removed every possible definition of sin from memory!"

The word 'remember' in Greek is *mimnesko*, meaning to call to mind, recall, and make mention! It is to mentally grasp something or to purposefully, actively, remember. It implies in its meaning to remember it with reward or punishment.

In other words, Abba is saying, "I will not recall your sin, I will not mention it, and I will have no memory of the fall or its consequences." Abba never had a problem with sin consciousness—mankind did. He sees us ALL in Christ—holy, righteous, blameless, justified, sinless, complete, perfect, and WHOLE!

> *And yet, religion talks about the fall and Adam as though they were existing issues.*
>
> *It fails to understand that God is not forgiving sins or making people holy today because Jesus purged ALL our sins, completely sanctified us—and He* **SAT DOWN!**

His sitting down is the equivalent of God rested on the 7th day (Genesis 2:2). God rested because everything, including Adam and Eve (who represented ALL mankind at the time), was FINISHED, perfect, and complete. And likewise, Jesus SAT DOWN because everything, including ALL mankind, is FINISHED, perfect, and complete. That's what Hebrews 1:3 says: when He had by Himself (no help from us) purged the sins and SAT DOWN. The word *by* is the word *dia*, meaning completely, successfully, 100% through Himself!

It was without our help then, now, or in the future! We do not purge ourselves from sin by restraining from what religion or our own conscience says is inappropriate activity. Of course, it's good to abstain from harmful things to yourself or others, but that's NOT purging sin. Only Jesus accomplished that.

And when He purged sin it was a complete
    FINISHED work.

The word 'purge' is *katharismos* in Greek, meaning cleansed. The root of the word means to make clean and pure and to declare clean and pure. Jesus not only *made* all mankind clean and pure; He also *declared* all mankind clean and pure. So why would we declare anything contrary to that?

Acts 10:15 says, "What the Lord has made clean don't regard as unclean!" And then, in verse 28, Peter said, "God has shown me that I should not call man (*anthropos* – mankind) unclean or impure."

So why are we still calling some unclean? Why are we still maintaining an "us and them" mentality when it comes to cleanness or purity?

God showed Peter not to call any man unclean or impure! Why? Because Jesus purged sin completely, successfully 100% by Himself, without our help. And He did it before you and I were ever born! So, from God's perspective, sin has never been an issue for you and me. It was only an issue for those who lived before the cross.

> Why was it never an issue for us? Because at the cross He purged ALL sin, made, and declared all men clean and pure, and then He SAT DOWN!

> His sitting down is the declaration of IT IS FINISHED!

Hebrews 9:26 says, "He put away ALL sin by the sacrifice of Himself." There are those words again... **by Himself.** And again, the word 'by' is *dia*, meaning completely, successfully, 100% by Himself, without our help. We must realize ALL truly is FINISHED. Sin was completely, successfully, 100% conquered, not just confronted! Sin has no power or authority over anyone! The only power sin has over anybody now is through deception, through lies.

> *But even then, it's an imaginary power, not a real power. It's not a power of substance.*

> *It's only a "power" that exists in a false, distorted "fallen mindset" of those who don't fully under-stand and embrace the FINISHED work of Jesus Christ and their identity IN Him.*

But remember, in Christ, the fall has been negated! There is no reason for us to relate to the fall of man in any way, shape, or form.

So, if the fall has been negated, and if from the Abba's perspective it is as though it never happened, then what else has been negated?

Everything that was a result of the fall was negated. That's good news!

Romans 5:12 tells us that sin entered the world through one man (Adam), and through sin, death entered the world. What is death? It encompasses everything that corrupts and spoils the human condition, existence, and experience. Sickness, disease, discouragement, depression, insanity, addiction, immorality, fear—ALL are part of death. The one word—death—describes everything contrary to human life.

Everything connected with sin and death has been eradicated! In other words, if sin doesn't exist, then sickness and disease don't exist. It's a simple understanding of cause and effect! Sin was the cause of sickness and disease, but once the cause is removed, the effect is automatically removed. We are already healed... We are already whole... nothing missing, nothing broken! That's the Gospel!

One morning as I was waking, I heard in my spirit the verse "He has quickened our physical bodies (Romans 8:11). And then Abba said, "Your physical body is alive with the Life of the Triune God (Father, Son, and Spirit). It is pulsing with the very Life of God."

When Jesus shouted *tetelestai* or IT IS FINISHED from the cross, it was a cry of victory! It was a declaration of the consummation of ALL things. He was declaring that the war or battle of mankind not knowing who they are and who God is—their struggle with sin and death—has ended! It's done, it's over! FINISHED!

In Revelation 21:5–6, John heard Jesus declare from the throne, "Behold, I make ALL things new. Write: for these words are faithful and true. It is DONE! I AM the Alpha and Omega, the Beginning and the End."

The word 'done' is *ginomai* in Greek means to emerge, to transition from one condition or one realm to another. It signifies a change of situation, state, or place. He had just said in verse 5, "Behold, I make ALL new!"

His FINISHED work changed everything!

He completely conquered sin and death. In Him, ALL of Adam died because ALL was FINISHED. ALL the effects of death were canceled—sickness, disease, poverty, fear, depression, addiction, etc. His FINISHED work reversed the effects of the fall.

His FINISHED work rescued mankind from the dominion of darkness (from sin and death as a result of mistaken identity) and brought us (past tense! FINISHED!) into the kingdom of His Son. IN Him, we are whole, complete, perfect, holy, righteous, justified, healed, prosperous, etc. IN Him, we have peace with God. We are face-to-face with God (Father, Son, and Spirit) in an intimate, unbreakable, indivisible union with Them. IN Him, we are filled with ALL the fullness of the Godhead.

IT IS DONE! ALL WAS MADE NEW! IT IS FINISHED! And the result is that we are WHOLE—nothing missing, nothing broken in our lives here and now.

Chapter 11

The Main Point part two

"By the which will we are sanctified through the offering of the body of Jesus Christ once for ALL. ^{11} And every priest stands daily ministering and offering oftentimes the same sacrifices, which can never take away sins: ^{12} But this Man, after He had offered one sacrifice for sins forever, SAT DOWN on the right hand of God; ^{13} From henceforth expecting till his enemies be made his footstool. ^{14} For by one offering he hath perfected forever them that ARE sanctified."
— Hebrews 10:10–14

In verse 10, the word 'by' is *en* which is translated in — it's a position of rest. So, it says, *in that will* we are sanctified (made holy). In what will? In verse 9, Jesus says, "I have come to do Your will." He's talking about the Father's will. So, IN the Father's will, through Jesus, we have been made holy! FINISHED!

What was Abba's will? In verse 9, it says, "He takes away (abolishes) the first, that the second may be established."

The Father's will was to completely do away with the sacrificial system of the Law through the final sacrifice of Jesus.

In verse 8, it says, "*Sacrifices and offerings, burnt offerings and sin offerings You did not desire, nor did You delight in them* (although they are offered according to the Law)." In the Father's will—which was the end to the Law's required sacrificial system—all humanity has been sanctified through the one sacrifice of Jesus.

We have been made holy, pure, blameless, set apart. The phrase "have been made" is in the perfect passive tense. Passive voice means it was ALL His doing. And perfect tense means an action completed in the past with results still occurring in the present. We are fully sanctified, and it was ALL His doing! The word "are" is in the present tense, meaning that it was completed. FINISHED!

In other words, we HAVE BEEN sanctified, and our sanctification is continuous and ongoing. We can't lose our sanctification because it was ALL His doing. He FINISHED it, and we remain sanctified IN Him because we were sanctified through the one offering of the body of Jesus.

It was entirely and successfully through His sacrifice. It didn't happen when we believed it—it was through His sacrifice alone. There was only one sacrifice, and it was for all time and for all people. It was once and for all! The writer of Hebrews said we are sanctified. Who is the "we" he is referring to? ALL humanity—John said in chapter 3 that the Father sent His Son because He loved the world.

> ALL mankind were sanctified completely, success-
> fully, 100% through the once-for-all sacrifice of
> Jesus.

So, what does the word 'sanctified' mean? It means to be made holy, to be set apart from and separated unto. Holy is a word we have misused and made into a religious term. We've linked it with "right" behavior. But that's not what holy means.

When we say God is holy, it means that He is set apart wholly unto us. Completely unto us. In other words, He's there for us all the time. He is set apart unto our love, care, and provision. He's never not there; He is always there with our welfare in mind. He's separated from every other god, every foreign god, and every inadequate, disabled god of our imagination. He's set apart unto us. That's holy.

When the Scripture talks about us being sanctified, it means He separated us from ALL Sin and Death.

> *He separated us from ALL that was corrupting our*
> *relationship with Him and destroying our experi-*
> *ence of the abundant life He created for us. And*

He set us apart unto Himself and His blessings,
unto His abundant life. That's holy.

So, it says in verse 10, "In that will, we have been sanctified." We—the whole world—have been sanctified through the offering of the body of Jesus Christ once for all. The whole world is holy unto God: separated from sin and set apart unto Him. Everyone is holy, blameless, and above reproach in the Abba's sight, all because of Jesus' sacrifice.

1 Corinthians 1:30 says, "It is because of Him that you are in Christ Jesus. He has become for us Wisdom, Righteousness, Sanctification, and Redemption."

Sanctification isn't a process — Sanctification is Jesus.

In Hebrews 10:11–12, it says, *"And every priest stands ministering daily and offering repeatedly the same sacrifices that can never take away sins. [12] **BUT** this Man, after He had offered one sacrifice for sins forever, sat down at the right hand of God."*

He is our High Priest who FOREVER SAT DOWN at the right hand of God—because He forever sanctified us.

Hebrews 10:13–14 says, *"From that time, waiting until His enemies were made a footstool. ¹⁴ For by ONE offering, He had perfected forever those who were being sanctified."*

So, according to this, God is not making people holy today. Why? Because He already did it once for ALL by the one sacrifice. How do we know this one sacrifice sanctified ALL? Because, in verse 11, it said that those Old Covenant priests had to daily stand ministering. Why did they have to stand? Because there was repetition involved. They couldn't sit down. Forgiveness of sins had to be done continually because they had to bring a sacrifice every time someone fell. Why? Because the Law's sacrificial system only covered sin, it didn't sanctify anyone! But Jesus' sacrifice, the one, perfect sacrifice, was different. How was it different? HE SAT DOWN. Why? Because we ALL have been made holy, perfected forever, and no other sacrifice would ever be needed! IT IS FINISHED!

Hebrews 10:14: *"For by one offering He has perfected forever those who are being sanctified. We have been perfected forever."*

The words "perfected forever" mean completed forever; FINISHED forever! Jesus offered the one sacrifice for ALL, and He SAT DOWN FOREVER because He perfected and completed those He sanctified — that is, ALL mankind. Remember, back in chapter 8, the writer of Hebrews told us that this is the main point—**He SAT DOWN!** The priests had to continually stand, offering sacrifices again and again.

This is what Abba is saying *in* and *by* His Son—our perfection and sanctification is FINISHED.

How do we know for sure? Because HE SAT DOWN! If we are still preaching that we need to ask God to forgive us, that we need to be purged from sin, that sanctification and perfection are a process, then we haven't heard what God the Father is saying *in* and *by* His Son.

> *He did it ALL, and He did it once for ALL — **and then He SAT DOWN FOREVER** because He completed, perfected, and sanctified ALL humanity for all time.*

But wait a minute, Robin, doesn't it say those being sanctified? Doesn't that mean it's a progressive sanctification?

The words 'being sanctified' use a present participle verb. It describes an action that is simultaneous with the action of the main verb. What is the main verb in this verse? PERFECTED! It is in the perfect tense, meaning it happened in the past, and the results continue in the future. In other words, when we were perfected—we were sanctified. It happened in one fell swoop!

When were we perfected? It says by His ONE offering!

And that happened two thousand years ago.

So, what does any of this in Hebrews have to do with healing? **EVERYTHING!** We need to understand New Testament healing, which isn't about needing continual healing but knowing that we are healed, knowing that we have no association with sickness and disease! Understanding that healing is a finished work. He did it once for ALL! And by His stripes, ALL were healed, made whole, and then He sat down! He bore our sicknesses and carried our diseases, and He sat down.

We pray, "Lord give me peace" because we don't grasp that the full chastisement of our peace was upon Him, and He sat down! If you're not at peace, it's because we haven't heard what the Father has spoken to us in and by His Son.

We may have heard preaching about it, but we haven't heard or understood what the Father has said *in* and *by* His Son—**"IT IS FINISHED!"—and He sat down!**

No one is being made righteous today! Why? Because the one act of righteousness resulted in the justification of life (righteousness) to ALL men (Romans 5:18). And Romans 4:25 says, "He was raised because of our justification." In other words, if we weren't justified or made righteous, then He'd still be in the grave. But the good news is that we can know we were ALL justified because He was raised from the grave! He's not making people righteous today because He did it once for ALL. There are no unrighteous people from God's perspective.

And yet, we continue to pray like David, asking God to purify our hearts or create in us a clean heart. Not understanding that He did it already once for ALL. As far as God is concerned, there are no unclean hearts, impure hearts. Because ALL humanity is pure and clean in Christ.

Jesus delivered, healed, justified, sanctified, prospered, and perfected ALL men for ALL time at the same time, **and He SAT DOWN forever! DONE! FINISHED!** The writer of Hebrews tells us that the main point or finality of all Abba said *in* and *by* His Son is that Jesus Christ is seated at His right hand forever. He will not rise again to perform additional works because ALL is FINISHED! This is the main point that we need to understand. We may not be experiencing it, but that doesn't change the reality that IT IS FINISHED, and He sat down forever. As we correctly *hear* this main point, this finality, we will begin to believe it. And then we will experience the benefits of what He FINISHED for us and *as us*!

Notice I said we will *experience* the benefits of it. We don't need to believe so we can BECOME righteous, perfect, holy, whole, etc. We believe it—we become fully persuaded of the reality of it—and then live in the experience of who we have always been from the Father, Son, and Spirit's perception.

Chapter 12

The Old Man Died

Paul is speaking to the church at Ephesus, those we would call today Christians or believers. He writes in Ephesians 4:17–18, "This I say, therefore, and testify in the Lord, that you should no longer walk as the rest of the Gentiles walk, in the futility of their mind, having their understanding darkened, being alienated from the life of God, because of the ignorance that is in them, because of the blindness of their heart."

The Mirror Bible offers a dynamic perspective: "My most urgent appeal to you in the Lord is this: you have nothing in common with the folly of the empty-minded masses; the days of conducting your lives and affairs in a meaningless way are over!"

Paul's message to the believers in Ephesus is clear: stop living in a meaningless way like the Gentiles, those who don't know God. Their understanding is darkened, and they are alienated from the life of God. This doesn't mean "separated from God," but rather that they are simply non-participants in the life of God. All humanity was created to be co-participators in God's life.

Their understanding is darkened because of the futility of their minds. God did not darken their understanding or alienate them. Their understanding is darkened because of the ignorance (the not knowing, or blindness) that is in them. And that blindness in them is because of the hardness of their hearts—their thoughts and feelings.

The word 'hardness' at its root means unperceptive, unresponsive.

They are blind to the truth of their identity because of their unperceptive and unresponsive thoughts and feelings. He's saying this is the way the Gentiles walk—unperceptive and unresponsive to God. And he tells these believers, these followers of Christ, that they are living life the same way—living life unperceptive and unresponsive to the life of God in them. Paul is contrasting the old man and the new man in these verses, using the example of believers and Gentiles or those who know God and those who don't yet.

The old man, the one who didn't know God, lived life in the futility of his mind. His understanding was darkened, and he was a non-participant in the life of God. He was blind because of the hardness of his heart—his thoughts and feelings. This old man was unperceptive and unresponsive to God.

The Mirror Bible captures it well: "The life of their design seems foreign to them because their minds are darkened through a hardened heart ruled by ignorance. They are blinded by the illusion of the senses as their only reference, stubbornly wearing a blindfold in broad daylight."

This was the old man before the cross.

The life he was designed for felt alien to him, and he
navigated his existence guided solely by his
senses.

Then Paul continues in verses 20–24, saying, "But you have not so learned Christ [21] if indeed you have heard Him and have been taught by Him as the truth is in Jesus [22] that you put off, concerning your former conduct (way of life; not just behaviors), the old man which grows corrupt according to the deceitful lusts (or simply corrupted by deception) [23] and be renewed in the spirit (attitude) of your mind (the way you think) [24] and that you put on the new man which was created according to God in true righteousness and holiness."

Contrary to popular teaching over the years, the old man is not who you were before asking Jesus into your heart. The old man Paul is referring to here is mankind before the cross. This old man had experienced all the effects of sin—death, sickness, disease, poverty, fear, and more. Paul is addressing a transitional generation that had emerged from under the Law. He's telling them that any association or identity with the old man is living life in the futility of the mind—living in emptiness, aimlessness, and lack of purpose. It is living as a non participant in the life of God

For us, born after the cross, we are not associated with the old man in any way, shape, or form because there is nothing left of Adam. ALL of Adam died and was buried with Christ, the Last Adam.

ALL the old man, ALL of Adam, and ALL that came because of sin —sickness, disease, poverty, fear—completely died two thousand years ago. None of Adam survived the cross! Now, we are free from anything that would keep us from living as co-participants in the life of God. As divine beings! As sons!

When this becomes our revelation, we will no longer yield to sickness, disease, poverty, fear, or addiction. We will understand that because sin was canceled, so was death, and therefore, ALL sickness and disease.

Again, the old man Paul refers to is not you before you asked Jesus into your heart.

The old man Paul refers to is mankind walking in the sense of 'Adamic' identity. Adam fell in his understanding of God's life in him, of the knowledge that he was a beloved son who reigned in grace. All men after him walked in that same fallen understanding. This is the old man that Paul talks about in his letters. He uses the term three times in Scripture—Romans 6:6; Ephesians 4:23–24; Colossians 3:9–10.

In Romans 6:6, it says, *"Knowing this, that our old man was crucified with Him, that the body of sin might be done away with, that we should no longer be slaves of sin."*

The Mirror Bible translates it as, *"We perceive that our old lifestyle was co-crucified together with Him; this concludes that the vehicle that accommodated sin in us was scrapped and rendered entirely useless. Our slavery to sin has come to an end."*

It finally clicked in my thinking a few years ago that because Adam (i.e., the old man) died on the cross, and because I was born on the FINISHED side of the cross, Paul was not referring to an old me and a new me. He's not referring to our life before accepting Christ as the old man and after receiving Christ as the new man. We have never had two different identities. We have never been slaves to sin! We were born righteous and free.

Someone may have lived a "sinful" life before coming into the knowledge of Christ, but they were never a slave to sin. Death and its effects of physical death, sickness, disease, poverty, etc., never had dominion over anyone born after the cross. Why? Because ALL were co-crucified and co-risen with Christ two thousand years ago.

The only way sin and death can "dominate" anyone is through wrong, distorted thinking. But even then, it is an illusory domination because sin and death have been defeated! FINISHED!

Romans 6:5 says, *"For if we have been united together in the likeness of His death, certainly we also shall be in the likeness of His resurrection."*

Please don't interpret the word "if" as conditional. Paul is not suggesting that our unity with Christ's death and resurrection is contingent on a specific moment, like asking Jesus into our hearts. Instead, he is affirming that we are already united with Christ in both His death and resurrection.

IF and THEN is Old Testament language.

New Testament language is FINISHED and DONE!

Paul told us in verses 3 and 4 that we were united with Christ in His death. In other words, because we were united in His death, we are also united in His resurrection. We are already in union with Him, based on His achievement. We are not the future bride of Christ who is spot-cleaning our wedding dress. No! Because we were united with Him in His death, we are now bone of His bone, flesh of His flesh. We are the new man, absolutely spotless and glorious now in this life.

Romans 6:6 says, *"For we know that our old self was crucified with Him that the body of sin would be done away with."*

We were never part of the body of sin because slavery to sin ended at the cross. In fact, the old man we have spent years trying to clean up has been dead for two thousand years. We have been trying to clean up, fix, and eliminate something that doesn't exist—a dead corpse.

We are not sinners saved by grace—we are the righteous, holy, and perfect new man in Christ. We
are just as sinless as Jesus is.

The gap between the facts—that we are dead, buried, and raised with Him—and our experience—living like it in this life is bridged by *knowing* some things. *Knowing* that the old man was crucified with Him and *knowing* that because Christ was raised from the dead, He dies no more. Death no longer has dominion over Him.

The word 'knowing' is *ginosko* in Greek. It is an intimately personal firsthand knowledge. It is heart-knowledge.

Our heart-knowledge of these things is the bridge between what God says is true and experiencing this truth in our daily lives. Romans 6:11 says, "Reckon yourself dead to sin and alive to God IN Christ Jesus!" We are fully alive IN Him! And because we co-died with Him, we are 100% completely dead to sin, death, sickness, disease, and everything else Adam introduced into the world through the fall.

Ephesians 4:22 says *"That you put off, concerning your former conduct, the old man which grows corrupt according to the deceitful lusts."*

The old man was humanity before the cross. It was their old sense of a fallen identity. Notice he doesn't say it was their nature or, as more commonly referred to by religion, a "sin nature." It was simply their former conduct of life. The old man was their former way of life, old behavior, old conversation, and the old way of seeing themselves, God, and the world around them. It was their old distorted, false sense of Adamic identity.

Paul's instructions are simply to put it off or lay it aside.

I like the Mirror Bible version: "Now you are free to strip off that old identity like a filthy worn-out garment. Lust corrupted you and cheated you into wearing it. (Just like an actor who wore a cloak for a specific role he had to interpret, the fake identity is no longer appropriate!)."

And the Passion translation adds, "And He has taught you to let go of the lifestyle of the ancient man, the old self-life, which was corrupted by sinful and deceitful desires that spring from delusions."

He said in verse 17 that they were to no longer walk in the futility of their mind, in their darkened understanding, being alienated from the life of God because of the blindness of their heart.

This is the old man.

This is mankind walking in the false, distorted sense of Adamic identity. They lived life in a meaningless way, their understanding was darkened, and they felt alienated from the life of God. They had lost their sense of purpose, forgetting they were sons made in the image and likeness of Abba. The old man lived unperceptive or unresponsive to God, blinded by a hardened heart (thoughts and feelings) veiled in unbelief.

The good news of the gospel is that the old man is absolutely dead, and one new man IN Christ resurrected with Him two thousand years ago. There is no old and new man, no Jew and Gentile, saved and unsaved, or righteous and unrighteous. However, not all men have this understanding yet. Not even all Christians have this under-standing! But regardless, ALL of Adam died and was buried with Christ (the Last Adam) two thousand years ago! And ALL of humanity resurrected with Christ as the new man—free from the bondage of sin and death, and free to walk in our renewed minds, which is the mind of Christ.

Ephesians 4:23–24 says, "*And be renewed in the spirit of your mind,* [24] *and that you put on the new man which was created according to God, in true righteousness and holiness.*"

The Mirror Bible says, "Be renewed in your innermost mind. (Ponder the truth about you, as it is displayed in Christ; begin with the fact of your co-seatedness.) This will cause you to be completely re-programmed in the way you think about your-self! [24] Immerse yourself into this God-shaped new person from above! You are created in the image and likeness of God. This is what righteousness and true holiness are all about."

So, in verse 23, he tells them (and us) to be renewed in the spirit of our mind, or to renew and reform our thinking. In other words, we are to ponder the truth about ourselves as it is displayed in Christ. We are to begin our pondering with our co-seatedness, living life here on earth from that position — co-seated with Him in heavenly places! We are to awaken to who we are as the new man, created in the image of God, righteous and holy.

It's not new as in the idea that it never existed. Genesis 1:27 tells us mankind was created in God's image and likeness. Mankind has always been righteous and holy because that's the image of God... *that's His nature!* It is new in the understanding that none of the old exists anymore.

The last verse that Paul talks about the old man is in Colossians 3:9–10.

> *"Do not lie to one another, since you have put off the old man with his deeds,* [10] *and have put on the new man who is renewed in knowledge according to the image of Him who created him."*

> The Mirror Bible translates verse 9 as, *"that old life was a lie, foreign to our design! Those garments of disguise are now thoroughly stripped off us in our understanding of our union with Christ in His death and resurrection. We are no longer obliged to live under the identity and rule of the robes we wore before; neither are we cheating anyone through false pretensions* (The garments an actor would wear define his part in the play but cannot define him)."

Colossians and Ephesians both tell us that our minds are renewed according to the image of God by putting on the new man. The phrase 'put on' means to sink into a garment. It signifies ceasing to struggle to become and simply resting in who we are—the image and likeness of God. It is realizing and resting in the truth that our right-eousness and holiness are complete and FINISHED in Christ. We don't have to try to attain anything or become more like Christ. We are to live as who He designed us to be—sons in His image and likeness.

Putting on the new man means being persuaded of who we are IN Christ.

It is recognizing that we are created like God, righteous and holy, made in His image and likeness. It is an awareness of only Christ, of oneness, of us in Him and Him in us. It is having no identification whatsoever with flesh and understanding that our identity is only Christ. He is ALL. He is ALL our life, ALL our righteousness, ALL our holiness. He is ALL our health, ALL our provision, ALL our obedience, and ALL our faith. Christ is ALL in ALL. ALL means ALL! There is nothing left out of ALL!

> I love verse 10 in the Mirror Bible, "*We stand fully identified in the new creation renewed in knowl-edge according to the pattern of the exact image of our Creator.*"

The old man was not the true design of mankind; it was not a sin nature that humanity possessed. It was a lie, foreign to our design. But now, we stand fully identified in the new creation. New doesn't mean we were given a new nature because the "sin nature" was removed. It is new in the sense that, as the old man, no one was free to walk in their true nature after Adam fell. Starting with fallen Adam, a distorted image was passed down to mankind, generation after generation. Remember, Ephesians 4:17 said that it was IN the futility of their minds that they walked.

It wasn't a "sin nature" they walked in but rather a futile mindset—a wrong, distorted way of thinking passed down generationally.

ALL the old man—all that came from Adam's fall (sin, death, sickness, disease, poverty, fear, etc.)—completely died at the cross. And now, ALL of mankind is free to walk in the revelation of the new man, our true, authentic self! We are free to see ourselves in the image and likeness of God, completely righteous and holy now. In verse 24, the phrase 'was created' is in the past tense, a FINISHED tense.

ALL mankind rose with Christ, born again a new man. FINISHED!

Chapter 13

Sickness & Disease Severed

The exodus story was written for our instruction so that we may have a confident expectation of victory in every area of our lives — an expectation of living life whole and complete!

Exodus 8:23 says, *"I will make a difference between My people and your people."*

The KJV says, *"I will put a division between My people and your people."*

The Hebrew word for 'division' is *peduth*, meaning ransom, redemption, and deliverance. The root of the word is *padah*, meaning to sever!

It says He will make a severing between My people and your people.
Who are Pharoah's people? The Egyptians, who are a type of death,
and all that death included: sickness, disease, poverty, fear, etc. God
is saying, "I'm going to put a division; I'm going to SEVER the association between My people and death! I'm going to sever the association
between My people and sickness and disease! I'm going to sever the
association between My people and lack of any kind." Who are
God's people? ALL mankind!

Another translation says, "I will set a Mediator
between My people and your people."

The Greek word for 'mediator' is mesites and means an agent
of goodness!

The New Testament tells us that Jesus is our Mediator. He is the
Agent of goodness. He completely put an end to sin, death, and ALL
sickness and disease. And as our Mediator, He's not just praying that
we make it through or praying that our faith is strong enough to get us
through sickness, disease, etc. No! His blood made an impassable
barrier between sin, death, sickness, disease, poverty, and more.
Those things cannot pass over to us! He is our Yahweh Rapha, the
Lord our Health, the Lord our Wholeness!

The Red Sea was a division, a severing between God's people and Egyptians. The Red Sea is a type of the blood of Christ.

The blood communicates the FINISHED work of Christ.

IT IS FINISHED is the division; it is the severing between us and sickness, disease, poverty, death, and more.

We've missed this truth by interpreting Egypt as a representation of the world, fostering an "us and them" mentality that caused us to see ourselves as divided or severed from the world. Egypt actually symbolizes sin.

He set His blood, the communication of IT IS FINISHED, as a division, a severing between us and death, sickness, disease, poverty, lack, and everything that came because of SIN. Exodus chapters 9 and 10 record the plagues that came upon Egypt but did not touch Israel. Death and all its attributes—sickness, disease, poverty, fear, etc.—could not touch them or anything that belonged to them. Darkness could not touch them. Why? Because God had made a distinction, a severing, between them and the Egyptians, a type of death.

Exodus 11:4–7 says, *"And Moses said, 'thus saith the LORD, "About midnight will I go out into the*

midst of Egypt: ⁵ And all the firstborn in the land
of Egypt shall die, from the firstborn of Pharaoh
that sitteth upon his throne, even unto the firstborn
of the maidservant that is behind the mill; and all
the firstborn of beasts. ⁶ And there shall be a great
cry throughout all the land of Egypt, such as there
was none like it, nor shall be like it anymore. ⁷ But
against none of the children of Israel shall not a
dog move his tongue, against man or beast: that ye
may know how that the LORD doth put a differ-
ence between the Egyptians and Israel.'"

None of these plagues touched the Israelites, making it clear that the LORD had severed the association between the Egyptians and Israel. Remember, Israel represents the world or ALL mankind, while the Egyptians symbolize death. In Exodus, God severed the association between the Egyptians and His people, Israel. For us, the association between death and all its attributes was severed from all of humanity.

He has severed ALL ties between us and any disease, circumstance, or situation we may be facing. He made a definitive separation between death and mankind.

This severing is forever—death has no dominion over Him, and it equally has no authority over us.

He severed the connection once and for all! He sees you whole in Christ, not bound to sin and death, because they were severed from humanity. They were done away with two thousand years ago. He made a division, a complete and final severing.

I know I'm repeating myself, but we must grasp this. If we don't understand this, we will continue to yield to sickness, disease, poverty, fear, and everything else that was introduced through the fall.

His severing death from ALL mankind allows us to dwell in perfect peace. It gives us certainty that 1,000 may fall at our side and 10,000 at our right hand, but it shall not come near us! It is the difference between poverty and wealth, between addiction and freedom, and between health and disease.

There's a tremendous, revelatory truth for us regarding our full, complete redemption in the story of the Exodus, particularly in chapter 14.

> **Exodus 14:10–14 says,** *"And when Pharaoh drew nigh, the children of Israel lifted up their eyes, and behold, the Egyptians marched after them; and they were sore afraid: and the children of Israel cried out unto the LORD. [11] And they said unto Moses, 'Because there were no graves in Egypt, hast thou taken us away to die in the wilderness? Wherefore hast thou dealt thus with us, to carry us forth out of Egypt?[12] Is not this the word that we did tell thee in Egypt, saying, "Let us alone, that*

we may serve the Egyptians?" For it had been
better for us to serve the Egyptians, than that we
should die in the wilderness.' ¹³ And Moses said
unto the people, 'Fear ye not, stand still, and see
the salvation of the LORD, which He will show to
you today: for the Egyptians whom you have seen
today, you shall see them again no more forever. ¹⁴
The LORD shall fight for you, and ye shall hold
your peace.'"

This takes place after Pharaoh released them, and now he's changed his mind and is pursuing them.

Their response to the enemy's pursuit is in verses 11 and 12. It says, "And they said unto Moses 'Because there were no graves in Egypt, hast thou taken us away to die in the wilderness? Wherefore hast thou dealt thus with us, to carry us forth out of Egypt? ¹² Is not this the word that we did tell thee in Egypt, saying, "Let us alone, that we may serve the Egyptians?" For it had been better for us to serve the Egyptians than that we should die in the wilderness.'"

They have a mental association with Egypt (a type of sin) that they haven't yet let go of. This new life of freedom doesn't come easily to their thinking. They still have a slave mentality. They still see slave life with the Egyptians as easier and better than this newly redeemed life they are unfamiliar with.

Moses' response to them is found in verses 13–14. He says, "Fear ye not, stand still, and see the salvation of the LORD, which he will show to you today: for the Egyptians whom you have seen today, ye shall see them again no more forever. ¹⁴ The LORD shall fight for you, and ye shall hold your peace."

He tells them to fear not and stand still. In other words, don't be afraid; just take your stand in the truth that you are no longer in Egypt, that you are no longer slaves, and see the reality of your salvation! They are seeing with their natural eyes the pursuit of the enemy. But Moses wants them to see, perceive, and understand the salvation of the Lord. He wants them to see that the Egyptians they see today, they will see NO MORE FOREVER!

Why wouldn't they see them again? Because the Egyptians were about to die in the Red Sea!

Remember, this story was written for our admonition, to guide our minds so that we might have a confident expectation of a victorious life! A confident expectation of FINISHED in every area of our lives! What is communicated to us in this story is that we are not to fear what looks like a pursuing enemy. We are to stand firm in the FINISHED truth that we are not slaves to sin and death. We have zero association or connection with sin and death.

We are to see and understand the *sozo* of the Lord — the FINISHED deliverance, healing, prosperity, and wholeness in every area, with nothing missing and nothing broken, that we have in Him. Because of the impassable sea of blood, because Jesus FINISHED all, we will see death, sickness, disease, poverty, and everything Adam introduced through the fall — **NO MORE FOREVER!**

Our natural eyes may think we see them pursuing us, but the reality is that they are dead on the seashore—dead on the cross.

Verse 30 says, *"Thus the LORD saved Israel that day out of the hand of the Egyptians (type of death), and Israel saw the Egyptians dead upon the seashore."*

Death, sickness, disease, poverty, addiction, and ALL that Adam introduced into the world through the fall are dead on the seashore. They died on the cross two thousand years ago!

Moses said in verse 14, "The LORD shall fight for you, and ye shall hold your peace." This was Moses talking to the children of Israel. Today, many still say, "the Lord will fight this battle for you" when referring to sickness. However, the truth is—HE ALREADY DID!

THE BATTLE IS OVER!

Jesus declared IT IS FINISHED (*tetelestai*), which means the conflict or war is over; lay down your weapons and go home! It's a declaration of peace! The Lord isn't fighting anyone's "battles" today. He is seated and at rest! And the good news is that we are co-seated with Him.

> In verses 26–27, it says, "*Then the Lord said to Moses,*
> "*Stretch out your hand over the sea, that the*
> *waters may come back upon the Egyptians, on*
> *their chariots, and on their horsemen.*" *27 And*
> *Moses stretched out his hand over the sea; and*
> *when the morning appeared, the sea returned to its*
> *full depth, while the Egyptians were fleeing into it.*
> *So the LORD overthrew the Egyptians in the*
> *midst of the sea.*"

Verse 27 declares that He overthrew the Egyptians (a symbol of death) in the midst of the sea (a representation of the blood of Christ).

The word 'overthrow' is naar in Hebrew, meaning to shake off. The root of the word is to growl like a lion—it paints a powerful picture of a lion rustling (shaking) his mane as he roars. Jesus, the Lion of Judah, roared IT IS FINISHED and shook off death along with ALL sickness, disease, poverty, and everything that resulted from the fall.

And verse 28 says, "And the waters returned and covered the chariots, the horsemen, and all the host of Pharaoh that came into the sea after them; not so much as one of them remained!"

Look at the last part of verse 28... *not so much as one of them remained!*

- **NOT DISEASE**
- **NOT SICKNESS**
- **NOT LACK**
- **NOT SIN**
- **NOT DEATH**
- **NOT A SINGLE EFFECT OF THE FALL REMAINED**

Why? Because ALL was swallowed up by the sea—by the blood of Jesus. 1 Corinthians 15:54 says death has been swallowed up in victory! The word 'remained' is shaar in Hebrew and means to be left over or to survive. It says nothing of death remained or survived. Death and ALL that came through death because of sin was COMPLETELY swallowed up by the blood of Jesus when He roared, "IT IS FINISHED!" Not one of them remained.

We must learn to see them dead on the cross and declare them dead on the cross. They were ALL overthrown in the blood of Jesus and rendered absolutely powerless.

Psalm 105:37 says, *"He also brought them out with silver and gold, and there was none feeble among His tribes."*

The word 'feeble' is *kashal*, meaning none were stumbling, staggering, bereaved, cast down, or caused to fail!

This passage is written for our instruction, to instill in us a confident expectation of victory and wholeness in every area of our life. He redeemed ALL mankind, and none were feeble. We must begin to believe that we are fully redeemed and not feeble, even when we "appear" to be stumbling, bereaved, cast down, or failing. We need to remember: He brought us out, redeemed us, and none are feeble!

Grasping the revelation that we were redeemed with a FINISHED, complete, whole redemption means understanding that we will never stumble, stagger, fall, or fail in life.

Psalm 106:10a says, *"And he saved them from the hand of him that hated them."*

Who was it that hated them? Egypt and the Egyptians—Sin and Death.

Verses 10b–11 continue, "And redeemed them from the hand of the enemy. 11 And the waters covered their enemies: there was not one of them left." Written hundreds of years after the Red Sea event, this psalm reflects a steadfast belief that not one of the Egyptians remained to pursue them. Verse 12 then says, "Then believed they His words; they sang His praise."

So, here's the thing: IF we've been redeemed—and we have—then it's a fact that the waters (the blood or FINISHED works of Jesus) have covered and destroyed our enemies (satan, sin, and death).

There is not one of them left! All of them, sickness and disease included, are dead upon the seashore now, today! Not one of them is left. The word "praise" means to tell the story! And this is the story we are to be telling: "Sickness and disease are dead on the seashore—none of it is left in my life!"

> Ezekiel 30:21–23 says, "*Son of man, I have broken the arm* (strength, force, and power) *of Pharaoh king of Egypt; and, lo, it shall not be bound up to be healed, to put a roller to bind it, to make it strong to hold the sword.*"

In this passage, Pharaoh represents Satan, the accuser, and Egypt symbolizes sin. Sin and the accuser of sin were destroyed two thousand years ago! Their strength, force, and power were COMPLETELY DESTROYED! Their arm was broken into pieces, crushed, and obliterated! Abba says that they—sin and the accuser of sin—would NOT be healed, bandaged, or even made strong enough to hold a sword (to use a weapon against you)! It was a COMPLETE defeat!!

Let's look at Deuteronomy 7:15 again. It says, "And the Lord will take away from you ALL sickness and will afflict you with NONE of the terrible diseases OF Egypt which you have known ~~but will lay those upon all those who hate you~~." (*Note: The latter part of the verse, which states "but will lay those upon all those who hate you," I put a line through as it does not reflect the heart and nature of God that we see in Jesus.*)

In this verse, God equates sickness and disease with Egypt, which symbolizes sin. Sickness and disease are thus connected to sin—not "sinful" behaviors, but the sin that Adam introduced into the world. This sin distorted our identity, our understanding of God, and our perception of the world, leading to the loss of our identity as sons.of self, God, and the world. It was the loss of the identity of sonship.

Through sin, death entered the world, bringing with it sickness, disease, poverty, and more. But now, mankind is no longer enslaved to sin. Hebrews 9:26 declares, "But now He has appeared once for all at the end of the ages to do away with sin by the sacrifice of Himself." His sacrifice did away with sin, rejecting and canceling it. According to Strong's Concordance, it rendered sin no longer in effect! The root word for canceled also means rejected.

Jesus rejected that fallen mindset, and when He died, sin died. ALL of Adam along with that fallen distorted mindset, that loss of the identity of sonship, died that day two thousand years ago!

Sin was rejected and canceled on the cross. It is no longer in effect! Sickness and disease were connected to death that came as a result of sin. But sin is NO LONGER in effect; therefore, death in all of its manifestations such as sickness and disease are NO LONGER in effect!

Matthew 2:15 says, "... out of Egypt I called My Son." Galatians 4:7 says, "We are all sons of God in Christ." Abba redeemed ALL His sons out of Egypt. He fully redeemed all humanity out of sin. And the first thing He did after bringing us out of sin, as we saw in Exodus 15, was to reveal His identity as our HEALTH and WHOLENESS, identifying us as healed and whole in Christ!

The word 'out of' is *ek* in Greek and is a preposition that speaks of origin and source.

Sin is not our origin. Sin is not our source. Abba is our Source! Egypt or sin was the false, distorted Adamic identity—the fallen mindset—that mankind, the old man, walked in. But we are not in sin. We are in Christ! And in Christ, we have been redeemed from Egypt or sin! Sin was canceled, it was rejected two thousand years ago.

This understanding is difficult for some to grasp or accept. Some will struggle with this and, at times, will be tempted to reject it because their experiences with sickness and disease contradict it. But the reality is that sin, death, sickness, disease—all the effects of the fall—were nailed to the cross and FINISHED two thousand years ago.

The problem is that we, as believers, don't understand the finality of FINISHED! We are always fluctuating in our thinking, judging life based on our circumstances rather than God's truth. For example, we judge our healing, prosperity, and deliverance by what we see happening around us.

We believe by His stripes we are healed because the Bible says so, BUT we also believe that if it's flu season, we can get sick, or that we will deteriorate as we age, or that if we aren't immunized, we might catch whatever is going around.

BUT God said NO MORE FOREVER!

All we need to do is rest in that reality, being fully persuaded that what Jesus FINISHED for us and as us, severed us from ALL sickness and disease. Physical disease is NOT of biological origin. It is connected only to sin—to the false distorted sense of identity.

But what about when someone with a virus breathes on you? Can't we catch what they have?

There are people who, because they understand the objective reality of our wholeness, can be exposed to any virus, and they won't catch anything.

During the plague in Africa, John G. Lake asked for a highly contagious bubonic plague virus to be poured on his hand. He wanted those around him to understand that the spirit of life in Christ Jesus had made him free from the law of sin and death. Scientists, observing through a microscope, saw that the organisms died instantly when they touched his hand.

How was that possible? Because he understood that he was completely redeemed from sin. He knew he had no association with sickness and disease. Therefore, it had no power over him. Why? Because sickness and disease are not of biological origin—all disease originated and sprang up from the condition called sin—the false, distorted, fallen Adamic sense of identity.

Most have a hard time believing it because their experiences contradict this truth. But don't let your experiences dictate what you believe. Don't let your experience become the authority of your body. The power of sickness and disease is only in connection with sin.

And the good news of the gospel is that everyone born after the cross was born free of sin. We were never enslaved or connected to sin; we were just taught that we were.

Hebrews 9:26 says, "He put away (canceled or rejected) sin by the sacrifice of Himself." He canceled and rejected sin and death by the sacrifice of Himself two thousand years ago!

It was canceled before we were ever born! In truth,
after the cross, mankind was never in Egypt (sin)
—we've always been in CHRIST.

Sickness and disease today come only through an assumed association or identification with sin. In other words, when we believe that we are still in some way connected to sin, we accept sickness and disease as a normal part of life.

So, how might we unknowingly associate or identify with sin in our daily lives?

We do this by still seeing ourselves as sinners saved by grace or by not seeing ourselves as fully, 100% justified and as completely sinless as Jesus. We also fall into this trap by not realizing that God is no longer imputing sin against anyone because Jesus is the Lamb who completely took away the sin of the world.

We fail to grasp the finality of Hebrews 10:2, which says, "Because that the worshippers once (once for ALL) cleansed should have had no more conscience of sins." When we truly understand that we are the righteousness of God in Christ, that there has been a full and complete exchange between Jesus and us—that we are fully redeemed from sin and death—we will declare, just like Jesus did in John 14:30, "The ruler of this world cometh but he has NOTHING in Me."

The illusion of sin, death, sickness, and disease has nothing in us— they have absolutely no power or authority in our lives

> Deuteronomy 7:15 says, *"The terrible diseases OF Egypt which you have known."*

Israel was familiar with the diseases of Egypt. Sickness and disease had been their experience while they were enslaved in Egypt. They likely died from disease, caught infections, suffered from contagious sicknesses, lost babies to childhood diseases, had miscarriages, etc. Because while they were in Egypt, they were engulfed in Egypt's life, they were enslaved to it.

So, it says, the terrible diseases OF Egypt (type of sin) which you have known. But then notice that God says, "But I (the Lord) will take away from you **all sickness**."

God said: I will take away from you ALL sickness. ALL! Not some, not just the big diseases. Not just the terminal diseases that the doctors can't find a cure for, leaving the small things like colds, flus, infections, and afflictions that are "manageable."

He said ALL!

And He was not saying that He would take away from them all sickness on a case-by-case basis by continually healing them when they would get sick. No! In both verses, Exodus 15 (I am the Lord who heals you) and Deuteronomy 7:15 (I will take away from you ALL sickness), what is being communicated is a completed, FINISHED work..

He's referring to a once and for all out of Egypt reality for them. And for us, it is communicating a once and for all out of sin reality, a full FINISHED redemption free of ALL sin, death, sickness, disease, lack, etc.

God wants us to embrace a higher vision, a co-seated perspective, understanding that He resurrected us in Christ to live now, in this world, free from ALL sickness and disease. Let's begin to see from that vantage point! Let's release our past experiences of sickness, disease, poverty, fear, anger, and more, and live in the revelation of wholeness in every area of our lives.

Because if we've left Egypt (sin)—and we have—and if God overthrew the Egyptians (death, sickness, disease, lack, etc.)—and He did—then we are 100% completely free of and SEVERED from ALL sickness and disease forever! FINISHED!

This is the gospel of Grace!

This is the 'almost too good to be true, radical, hyper, offensive to our sensibilities, contradicting everything we've been familiar with,' grace of God IN Christ.

Chapter 14

Free From the Curse of the Law

Galatians 3:1–14 says, *"O foolish Galatians! Who has bewitched you? Before your very eyes Jesus Christ was clearly portrayed as crucified. ² I would like to learn just one thing from you: Did you receive the Spirit by works of the law, or by hearing with faith? ³ Are you so foolish? After starting in the Spirit, are you now finishing in the flesh? ⁴ Have you suffered so much for nothing, if it really was for nothing? ⁵ Does God lavish His Spirit on you and work miracles among you because you practice the law, or because you hear and believe? ⁶ So also, 'Abraham believed God, and it was credited to him as righteousness.' ⁷ Understand, then, that those who have faith are the sons of Abraham. ⁸The Scripture foresaw that God would justify the Gentiles by faith and preached the gospel to Abraham: 'All nations will be blessed through you.' ⁹ So those who have faith are blessed along with believing Abraham ¹⁰ All who rely on works of the law are under a curse. For it is written: 'Cursed is everyone who does not continue to do everything written in the Book of the Law.' ¹¹ And it is clear that no one is justified before God by the law, because 'The righteous will live by faith.' ¹² The law, however, is not based on faith; on the contrary, 'The man who does these things will live by them.' ¹³*

Christ redeemed us from the curse of the law by becoming a curse for us. For it is written: 'Cursed is everyone who is hung on a tree.' ¹⁴ He redeemed us in order that the blessing promised to Abraham would come to the Gentiles in Christ Jesus, so that by faith we might receive the promise of the Spirit."

F irst, let's clarify that the Law was never intended for the Gentiles. It was specifically for the Jews and only for a limited period—it had an expiration date. The Law was given through Moses to the children of Israel until Christ came. Today, no one is under the Law, not even the Jews. Unless you were Jewish and lived during the period from Moses' giving of the Law at Mt. Sinai until the cross, you were never under the Law.

Unfortunately, a significant portion of the body of Christ still views the Law and the Ten Commandments as our standard or moral compass for holiness. This misunderstanding prevents us from grasping that Galatians 3:14 addresses two distinct groups: Jews and Gentiles.

Galatians 3:14 says, *"He redeemed us so that the blessing promised to Abraham would come to the Gentiles in Christ Jesus so that by faith we might receive the promise of the Spirit."*

Paul said that Christ redeemed "us." We've been taught that Paul is addressing "us" in the church, but Paul is specifically speaking to the Jews who had been under the Old Covenant, under the Mosaic Law.

They were redeemed so that the blessing promised to Abraham would come to the Gentiles IN Christ. ALL mankind was redeemed, but in this verse, Paul focuses on the Jews being redeemed from the Mosaic Law.

It's important to know who the verses refer to and note that for future reference.

> Colossians 2:14 says, *"Blotting out the handwriting of ordinances* (Old Mosaic Law) *that was against us* (the Jews under that Law), *which was contrary to us* (again, Jews under the Law) *and took it out of the way, nailing it to the cross."* [emphasis mine]

He redeemed those under the Law so that the Gentiles (all mankind who wasn't a Jew) would receive the promise of the Spirit. And He made ONE new man out of the two—Jew and Gentile—in Christ—no division! Ephesians 2:14 says, "For He Himself is our peace, who made both groups into one and broke down the barrier of the dividing wall."

> ALL men born after the cross were simply born in the freedom of life in the Spirit, of Christ in us, with no connection to the Mosaic Law whatsoever.

Two thousand years should've produced generations of people who are fully walking in this newness of life. But mentally, the church has placed itself under a Law that no longer exists and was never for us. And mentally, as believers, we have seen ourselves redeemed from curses that never applied to us.

Most believers mistakenly link Galatians 3:13 with the extensive list of curses in Deuteronomy 28:16-68. But notice the difference: Deuteronomy talks about curses (plural), whereas Paul in Galatians mentions a singular curse. He specifically refers to "the curse," not "the curses."

What was this singular curse? It was the curse of the Law—the harsh reality that the Law, while exposing humanity's broken condition, held no power to justify or transform anyone. Its purpose was to lead us to Christ, to make us aware of our need for Him, but it could not change us.

Paul, speaking to the Jews, says in Romans 7:7, "What shall we say then? Is the law sin? Certainly not! On the contrary, I wouldn't have known sin." Notice, the word 'sin' here is singular, not plural. He's not referring to behaviors. He is addressing the false, distorted Adamic identity—the sin that was introduced into the world.

Romans 3:20 says, *"Therefore by the deeds of the Law
no flesh will be justified in His sight for by the
Law is the knowledge of sin."*

Notice again, the word 'sin' is singular. Paul is telling the Jews they needed the Law to reveal the condition of sin—their distorted, false understanding of themselves, of God, and of their world. The Law wasn't given to make them righteous; it was designed to reveal their condition apart from the glorious gospel and point them to Christ.

Later in Galatians, in verse 21, Paul says the Law could not give life. And in verse 23, he tells them (still speaking to the Jews) they were kept under the Law or held in custody to the Law.

The word 'kept' or 'held in custody' is an imperfect indicative passive tense, meaning it was a repeated, continual action in the past that happened to them.

Paul is emphasizing that they are no longer held in custody or kept under the Law. It was a repeated action of the past, before the cross. But it's not their life anymore!

In verse 24, Paul tells them (not us!) that the Law was a trainer or tutor until Christ came. Then, in verse 25, he says that now that faith has come, they are free from the Law.

Whose faith is Paul talking about? He's not referring to their faith in Jesus or our faith in Jesus. Verse 22 makes it clear—it's the faith OF Jesus!

The Law was their tutor, their guardian, meant to bring them to Christ so that they would be justified by His faith. The Law was not a curse. In fact, in Romans, Paul says the Law is holy, righteous, and good. It was a tutor to lead them to Christ, to point them to the Gospel.

And so, the curse of the Law was that it couldn't justify them! The Law was never intended to be a guide for their flesh. In other words, it wasn't meant to teach them how to manage their behavior. Its sole purpose was to reveal the cause of ALL problems in the flesh.

What was the cause of ALL problems in the flesh?

The Sin—the false, distorted identity of living out of context with our original design, which is being sons made in the image and likeness of God.

That's why I've been telling you from the beginning of this book that disease is not of biological origin. It manifests biologically, but sickness and disease always have a spiritual origin. It's the experience of who we believe we are. It's easy to walk in divine health. It's easy to live whole and complete. But to do that, we must first grasp this revelation—that we have been fully redeemed from sin!

When we understand that we have been COMPLETELY delivered from sin, we can then understand that there is no negative effect of death without sin—and all that came with death—sickness, disease, etc. Sin entered the world through one man and death through sin; therefore, all died because all sinned. This cause-and-effect relationship communicates that when the cause is negated, the effect from the cause is also negated. In other words, no sin equals no death. Sickness and disease are only possible when we assume we are still in some way connected with sin. Hebrews 10:2 tells us that we're to have no more consciousness of sin because we have been purified!

Again, when we say sin, we're not talking about "sinful behaviors." We're talking about the false, distorted identity of living out of context with our original design, which is as beloved sons made in the image and likeness of God as lords on the earth.

Once we grasp the revelation that we have been completely 100% separated or severed from sin, then it becomes easier and easier to live in the experience of health, peace, joy, and prosperity. Because we realize that death and ALL its effects (sickness, disease, lack, etc.) were done away with when the cause (sin) was canceled or rejected by Jesus two thousand years ago!

Deuteronomy 28:15 says, *"But it shall come to pass, if thou wilt not hearken unto the voice of the*

> LORD *thy God, to observe to do all his command-*
> *ments and his statutes which I command thee this*
> *day; that all these curses* (plural) *shall come upon*
> *thee and overtake thee."*

Notice that verse 15 mentions curses (plural). Then the curses
(plural) are listed in verses 16–68. The entire rest of the chapter
relates to these curses (plural)—the natural corruption resulting from
breaking the Law.

Just like sin (the false, distorted identity) is singular and responsible
for sins (plural), the behavior that flows out of the distorted identity,
we need to realize that the curse is singular and responsible for the
curses. The curses flow out of the Curse.

The curses include all the natural corruption—sickness, disease,
poverty, marital distress, family disorder, social injustice, and more—
everything listed in Deuteronomy 28:15–68. However, we (all
humanity born after the cross) were never under the curse. It only
applied to the Jews from the period of Moses to Christ.

But because we've been taught that we were redeemed from the
curse, let's examine what it means to be redeemed from the curse "as
though it applied to us." This way, we can fully grasp the wholeness
that is ours IN CHRIST.

For the remainder of the chapter, I'm going to capitalize the words "Curse," "Death," and "Sin," and precede them with the article "the" to emphasize their specific and singular nature.

Understanding that we're only redeemed from the "things" listed in Deuteronomy 28:15–68, or from the curses (plural), is an incomplete revelation of our redemption. Defining the Curse solely by its natural effects or corruptions (curses) reduces Christ's work to merely a natural, physical ministry.

In other words, it implies that Christ's sacrifice only impacts the physical, earthly experience of men. This dramatically lessens the value of the cross and detracts from the revelation of the FINISHED work of Christ in its fullness. For instance, if Christ had only died for our sins (plural—referring to the behavior that flows out of a distorted identity), then we're forgiven but left unchanged! In that scenario, He did nothing for our spiritual condition, leaving us still lost and enslaved to a fallen mindset of a distorted, false identity.

Take Israel before the cross as an example: they had forgiveness of sins, yet they were still lost at that point in time. They were still in bondage to the Sin (singular—the fallen mindset; the false, distorted Adamic identity).

If Jesus only died for our sins (plural—referring to behavior), we're still lost and unchanged. The best we can hope for is a sense of forgiveness in this life.

This is exactly what the Law provided for the Israelites. Like them, we will never experience freedom from our constant self-imposed need for forgiveness if we have only been forgiven. However, if Jesus became the Sin—and He did!—we can experience freedom from that sin consciousness that continually demands forgiveness in our life.

Hebrews 9:14 says, *"HOW MUCH MORE shall the blood of Christ, who through the eternal Spirit, offered Himself without spot to God, purge your conscience from dead works to serve the living God?"* [emphasis mine]

The Mirror Bible translates it as, *"How much more effective was the blood of Christ, when He presented His own flawless life through the eternal Spirit before God, in order to purge your conscience from its frustration under the cul-de-sac rituals of the law. There is no comparison between a guilt and duty-driven, dead religious system, and the vibrancy of living your life free from a sin-consciousness! This is what the new testament priesthood is all about!"*

There was MUCH MORE needed than just the sanctifying and purifying of the flesh that the Law provided (verse 13). If all we have is forgiveness of sins (plural—behavior) and redemption from the curses (plural), we have nothing more than what Israel had. They had forgiveness of sins (plural—behavior) through sacrificial offerings. Verse 13 tells us that these sacrifices even purified their flesh. There were healing ordinances throughout the Old Covenant, throughout the Mosaic Law, that provided for their natural man.

> God, under the Old Covenant and the Mosaic Law,
> provided for their physical well-being.

By reducing Christ's redeeming us from the Curse (singular) of the Law to merely being redeemed from all those curses (plural) recorded in Deuteronomy 28, we don't have anything better than Israel had.

But the good news of the Gospel is that we have the MUCH MORE!

We're not just redeemed from the curses (plural); we are redeemed from the Curse! Just like we were not just forgiven of sins (plural); we were redeemed from the Sin. The Curse was responsible for the curses (cause and effect), just as the Sin was responsible for sins (behavior).

> Deuteronomy 30:19 (NKJV) says, *"I call heaven and earth to record this day against you that I have set before you, life, and death, blessing, and cursing: therefore, choose life, that both thou and thy seed may live."*

This version says blessing and cursing, but in Hebrew, it literally says *the* Blessing and *the* Curse. It's not talking about blessings and curses (plural); it is singular and specific! The verse also says the Life and the Death. Again, it's singular and specific.

Then it says, "choose life, that both you and your descendants will live."

Notice that it doesn't say we are to choose just any life; it points back to that singular specific Life—THE LIFE. In other words, the Blessing, the *Zoe* life—God's life. Because in choosing the Life, it says you and your descendants will live!

The words 'will live' is zao in the Greek Septuagint, and its definitions include: to enjoy real life, living water, to have vital power in itself and exerting the same upon the soul, to be strong, full of vigor, powerful!

Choosing the Life would cause them and their generations to live the abundant, very good, FINISHED Life! That Life is a vital power in them that affects their soul, mind, heart, will, emotions, conscience, etc. By choosing *the* Life, their experience would be abundant life and not the manifestations of the Death — sickness, disease, poverty, lack, fear, etc.

So, very clearly, we see that the Blessing is Life, and the Curse is Death. They are singular and specific—conditions of existence, not objects of reward and punishment. We often refer to blessings as objects of reward. For example, when we receive something, we call it a blessing. Actually, those things are the fruit of the Blessing. What we need to understand is that these terms describe a condition of existence—a state in which we are meant to live and dwell.

Before the cross, this condition was called the Death or the Curse. Now, from God's perspective, we eternally dwell in the Life or the Blessing.

---

1 John 5:12 says, "He that hath the Son hath the Life." We could also say he who has the Son has the Blessing. Again, when John speaks of the Curse and the Blessing here, he's not talking about rewards or punishments, but a condition of existence. Just as the Sin and the Death were conditions of existence, so were the Curse and the Blessing. The Curse on humanity was the Death, and the curses (plural) were the natural effects or corruptions of a spiritual root. They were men's natural experiences that resulted from the Curse or the Death.

That's why sickness and disease are not of biological origin. And why poverty and lack do not originate in the economy or your job.

They are all the effects of the Death or the Curse.

So, the Curse on humanity was the Death, and the curses were the natural corruptions of this spiritual root called the Death. We, as believers, haven't gone far enough in our understanding. We haven't grasped the finality of His FINISHED work and what that means for us. It means wholeness in every area of our lives, being filled with ALL the fullness of the Godhead, and being empowered to live in the realm of the spirit or the heavenlies.

And it's ALL NOW in this earthly life!

In Galatians 3:13, it does not say that Christ has redeemed us from the curses (plural), having borne the curses (plural) on His body on the cross. It says, "Christ has redeemed us from the Curse, having become the Curse." Christ becoming the Curse meant He became ALL of the Death, just like He became ALL of the Sin. In other words, He became ALL the Death so that ALL of His Life could become your only condition, your only existence. Just like He became ALL the Sin so that ALL of His Righteousness could become your only condition and existence. He became ALL the Sin and the Death, and we became ALL the Righteousness and the Life. We became only ALL Blessed!

He redeemed us from a condition, not from things.

He redeemed us from the Curse. He did not redeem us from sickness, disease, lack, etc. Because He redeemed us from the Curse, from the Death, there are no curses that remain. No sickness, no disease, no poverty, etc., none of the curses from Deuteronomy remain because He redeemed us from the Curse, from the Death.

Our condition now is only the Life of God, only the BLESSING. This is the condition of our existence, whether we know it or not, and whether we believe it or not. You're not blessed because you get things. You're blessed because you have the Life. And because you have the Life, you live in this place called the Blessing. They're synonymous. And in that place (Paul calls it our NEW LIFE IN Christ), there is NO SICKNESS, NO DISEASE, NO LACK, NO FEAR, ETC.

Matthew 3:10 says, *"And now also the ax is laid unto the root of the trees: therefore, every tree which bringeth not forth good fruit is hewn down and cast into the fire."*

This isn't talking about people who aren't bearing good fruit. People aren't cut down, wholly removed, severed, and thrown into the fire. It's not about God destroying some people who aren't bearing the right fruit in their lives. That kind of thinking produces fear in people, which ironically, is not good fruit!

Matthew 3:10 says the ax is about to be laid to the root (singular and specific) of the trees (plural and distinct). I like that the word 'laid' has as its root meaning to be outstretched. Jesus was outstretched on that cross, and He went right to the root or the source of those two trees. And that source is not your bad behavior.

The trees He's referring to here are the Sin and the
Death.

Notice it says that the ax is laid to the root (singular) of the trees
(plural). What is the root? The Sin is the root of both trees. Romans
5:12 says, "*The Sin* entered the world through one man and then *the
Death* through *the Sin*" [emphasis mine]. The Death is one of those
sucker trees that grow out of the root and grows from the root of the
original tree. If it's not pruned off, it becomes a second tree. And that's
precisely what happened: the Sin (singular) sprung up, and the
Death (singular) grew right out of that root into a second tree.

Jesus came and put the ax to the single root of those
two trees.

It says every tree is cut down and thrown into the fire. The trees were
thrown into the fire. Consequently, the fruit that grows from those
trees was also destroyed. Fruit cannot survive without the tree. But
we've resurrected the fruits in our thinking. Remember all those dead
Egyptians on the seashore? They were a type of the fruit of the
Death. They were all dead on the seashore. All the effects or fruit
(the natural corruption) of the tree of the Death, which came through
the Sin, were ALL dead on the cross. This includes things like sickness, disease, poverty, lack, fear, etc. They were ALL thrown into the
fire along with the trees!

But in the body of Christ, we've revived them in our
   minds.

We've tolerated sickness and disease in our lives instead of living by
the truth of what God says. We've allowed our experiences, what the
media says, and what other people believe to determine our expectations. For example, we're taught to expect sickness and disease as we
get older. We're taught it's part of our natural DNA—if our parents or
grandparents had it, we will too. We're taught that the foods we eat,
the beverages we drink, and the air we breathe can negatively affect
our health, causing sickness and disease.

NO! ALL sickness and disease were dead on the seashore—dead on
the cross.

They can only live if we revive them with our breath. In other words,
by speaking that as our expectation in life. That's the only way it can
live in our lives anymore. The effects of the Death (sickness, disease,
lack, fear, etc.) are not of biological (natural) origin. They have a spiritual origin, only connected to the Sin (the false, distorted identity).

Deuteronomy 7:15 says, "The LORD will remove from you ALL
sickness, and He will not put on you any of the harmful diseases of
Egypt which you have known." Egypt is a type of the Sin. And
Hebrews 9:26 says, "He appeared to put away the Sin by the sacrifice
of Himself." The Greek says "the Sin" or "the hamartia"—singular and
specific. It speaks of the fallen condition of men's minds, not the
wrong behaviors we call sins. The words 'put away' mean canceled,
rejected, and rendered no longer in effect!

Sin is no longer in effect; there is only the condition of righteousness now.

Romans 5:18 says, "So, then, as through one offense to ALL men it is to condemnation, so also through one declaration of 'Righteous' it is to ALL men to justification of life." There is only one declaration—Righteous! ALL men are justified! The word justified means pronounced righteous, and to be sinless, never connected to the Sin!

Now, ALL mankind's condition is abundant *zoe* life—righteousness, blessed, and free from any trace of the Sin. This is our new, eternal reality!

It's the same situation here in Matthew 3:10. The fruit of the trees were thrown into the fire with the trees. If the trees are cut off at the root, there is no longer a source to produce the bad fruits of sickness, disease, poverty, fear, addiction, etc. You are free! You were born free in Christ!

The only tree in your life is the Tree of Life that lives within you, and its fruit is wholeness and health in every area of your life!

Part Three

Living A Healed Life

Here in part three, I want to take time in these last seven chapters to discuss revelations that can help us live life in the FINISHED work of our restored health and wholeness.

None of these chapters are in any particular order. And they are definitely individual studies that could in themselves be entire books. I merely give them to you as jumping-off points for you to do your own further studies.

Chapter 15

Paul's Thorn in the Flesh

Paul's thorn in the flesh is often misunderstood and misinterpreted. It's crucial to recognize that his thorn wasn't a physical illness but rather the relentless persecution and opposition he encountered. The message Paul carried was revolutionary, shaking the foundations of both religious and societal norms.

Paul was chosen to bring the message of grace, freedom, and divine health to both Jews and Gentiles. This message threatened established religious institutions and societal structures. His thorn was a metaphor for the continuous harassment and hardships imposed by those opposing his ministry.

The idea that Paul's thorn was a sickness comes from a misreading of the text and an underestimation of the spiritual and physical battles Paul faced. His adversaries—both spiritual and human—were the thorns that sought to hinder his mission. Understanding this context is key to comprehending the true nature of Paul's struggles.

Recognizing Paul's thorn as persecution, not sickness, reinforces the truth that sickness and disease are not part of God's plan for us. We are called to live in divine health, free from the bondage of illness. Paul's endurance amidst persecution exemplifies the strength we can find in Christ.

In 2 Corinthians 1:8, Paul shares, "*For we do not want you to be ignorant, brethren, of our trouble which came to us in Asia: that we were burdened beyond measure, above strength, so that we despaired even of life.*"

This passage highlights the intense troubles Paul faced, so overwhelming that he "even despaired of life." But let's be clear: this doesn't mean Paul wanted to die or that he had given up hope, thinking death was God's will for him.

The Mirror Bible captures this sentiment perfectly:
"*We really thought we were going to die.*"

Then, in verse 9b, Paul adds, "*... there was no escape except our belief that God could raise us from the dead.*"

Paul's faith in the resurrection power of God was unwavering. He knew that even if they tried to kill him, God could raise him from the dead. Paul was not giving up hope or desiring death; he was expressing the magnitude of his trials and his steadfast belief in God's power to deliver him.

Then, in 2 Corinthians 12, we find Paul praying for God to take away the thorn in his flesh. He wasn't asking God to remove sickness from him. Thorns in the Bible often symbolize persecutions and troubles, not physical ailments.

Numbers 33:55 uses a similar phrase: "pricks in your eyes and thorns in your sides." The Septuagint translates this as "a thorn in your eyes and a dart in your side." The word 'eyes' in Greek is "opthalmos," which literally means the eye but is also used metaphorically to refer to the eyes of the mind or the faculty of understanding.

> The enemy in the Promised Land was a thorn in
> Israel's understanding, a thorn in their
> perception.

We see this when the spies returned, reporting that they saw themselves as grasshoppers in the eyes of their enemies. This perception caused a thorn in their understanding. They saw themselves not as they truly were but as they imagined their enemies saw them.

And in Joshua 23:11-13, we see the phrase "thorns in your eyes" again. Joshua is about to die, and these are his final words to the Israelites. He's telling them that they will possess the Promised Land because Yahweh, I AM, will drive out their enemies, and no one and nothing will stand against them. Then he instructs them not to go back and cling to those enemies, nor to make marriages with them.

In other words, don't turn back and be joined to those defeated enemies again.

Joshua warns that if they do, these defeated enemies will become snares, traps, scourges in their sides, and thorns in their eyes or perception. They would perish from this good land that I AM has given them. The word 'perish' in the Septuagint is the Greek word *apollymi* and means to lose and render useless. The Hebrew word means to wander away.

When we join ourselves or identify with anything Jesus defeated, such as sickness, disease, sin, death, etc., it causes us to wander away from the very good land of IT IS FINISHED. It is a thorn in our eyes... a distorted perception and understanding of living a FINISHED life.

Those thorns in our eyes or in our flesh hinder our enjoyment of living life whole and complete. They distort our perception and keep us from fully grasping the reality of our freedom and wholeness in Christ. When we understand that these thorns represent the enemy's attempts to distort our perception, we can better appreciate that Paul's thorn was not a physical ailment but the relentless persecution and opposition he faced. This perspective shift helps us see that we, too, can overcome these thorns by aligning our perception with the truth of our completed redemption in Christ.

This idea is repeated in Judges 2:2–3 and Ezekiel 28:24. Both passages talk about Israel's victory and restoration, emphasizing that there would be NO MORE thorns in their side nor those around who despise them. The phrase, "... those around who despise them," is translated as "thorns of consuming grief, pains, and sorrow" in the Septuagint. Why will there be no thorns of consuming grief, pain, and sorrow in their lives? Because they shall intimately, personally know Yahweh, or I AM! We more than know I AM. We personally, intimately, *know* Him. We are *one* with Him. And *in* Him, we have complete victory over ALL distorted perceptions, consuming grief, pains, and sorrows.

The Mirror Bible translates 2 Corinthians 12:7–8 beautifully:

> *"In sharp contrast to these spiritual revelations, the*
> *physical pain that I suffered, and my severe*
> *discomfort momentarily distracted me. It was as if*
> *the old mindset of accusation* [satan] *persuaded*
> *me that this affliction was actually God's way of*
> *keeping me humble. [8] I almost believed this lie*
> *and even implored the Lord three times to remove*
> *the thorn from my flesh."*

This translation highlights the spiritual struggle Paul faced, showing that his thorn was not a physical ailment but a mental and emotional battle against the old mindset of accusation. Understanding this helps

us see that we, too, can overcome these thorns by aligning our perception with the truth of our completed redemption in Christ.

In Exodus 14:15–16, we see Moses, like Paul, asking for God to do
something He's already done. God's response to Moses was, "Why do
you cry to Me for help?" In other words, He is saying, "All that you
need I have already done for you, all that you think you need, I have
already given you." Similarly, Abba's response to Paul's thorn in the
flesh was, "My grace is sufficient for you!"

> The Mirror Bible puts it beautifully, "*Finally it
> dawned on me that grace is God's language; He
> doesn't speak 'thorn-language!' He said to me, 'My
> grace elevates you to be fully content.' And now,
> instead of being overwhelmed with a sense of my
> own weakness, he overwhelms me with an aware-
> ness of his strength! Oh, what bliss to rejoice in the
> fact that in the midst of my frailties I encounter
> the dynamic of the grace of God to be my
> habitation!*"

Jesus suffered a crown of thorns for us, as us! He bore every thorn for
us, as us! His suffering is our co-suffering. The word 'sufficient' in
Greek is arkeo and means keep off, enough, or suffices; it carries the
idea of raising a barrier or removing. Jesus is Grace! He is our barrier!
Grace is enough! And Grace removed the thorns!

He removed the distorted perceptions that Adam passed down to mankind, the consuming griefs, pains, and sorrows. He removed sin and death and all that came with them—sickness, disease, fear, addiction, lack, poverty, etc.

Grace is our Barrier! He is our Sufficiency!

Even when it doesn't look like it to our natural eyes, or when we're tempted, like Paul, to believe the lie by listening to that old voice of accusation trying to persuade us this circumstance is God's way of keeping us humble, testing us, or punishing us. The writer of Hebrews 2 tells us the authority we have over ALL things, and then he says, "But we see Jesus!" When it doesn't look like we're victorious or have authority over ALL things, we just need to see Jesus. Because in beholding Him, we see ourselves. And in chapter 1 of Hebrews, we are told that God has spoken to us in and by His Son.

What did the Son say? IT IS FINISHED! He FINISHED it ALL— and every thorn was removed!

Paul's thorn in the flesh wasn't sickness or disease! The thorn was the persecutions and afflictions that he went through with the religious Jews and the pagan rulers of his day. In chapter 11, he talks about his sufferings. He mentions physical beatings, imprisonment, being left for dead, and receiving 39 lashes on five different occasions. He was beaten with rods, stoned once, shipwrecked three times, and often faced dangers in the water. He experienced these sufferings from robbers, his own countrymen, and the Gentiles. They happened in the city, in the wilderness, in the sea, among false brethren, in weariness and toil, and often in sleeplessness, hunger, thirst, fasting, cold, and nakedness. And then he added to that list: there was also the daily pressure of his concern for all the churches.

Nowhere do we read that he was sick or suffering from a disease.

Because of the message he proclaimed and lived, Paul suffered affliction and persecution from religious and political leaders. But Paul had the promise of Luke 10:19: "He has given us authority to trample on snakes and scorpions and upon ALL the power of the enemy."

The Greek word for 'enemy,' *echthros*, means someone openly hostile, driven by deep-seated hatred, and an adversary bent on inflicting harm.

Paul's victory during these trials came from his conscious awareness of the life of Christ IN him.

In 2 Corinthians 4, we read Paul's declaration about himself and us during times of seeming contradictions.

Here's my paraphrase of 2 Corinthians 4:8-9 based on Greek definitions:

"We may feel hard-pressed on every side, hemmed in,
under pressure, kept in suspense in the mind, and
distressed on every side, yet we are not crushed!
We don't make room for these things, hold on to
them, or progress in them. We may feel
perplexed, thinking we are in doubt, at a loss,
with no seeming way out. But we are not in
despair! This perplexing and despair are not from
within us... doubt, loss, and hopelessness are not
our life in Christ. We may be persecuted, feeling
pursued and hunted down by hostile adversaries
determined to harm us. But we are not forsaken.
We are not abandoned, deserted, or left in a
condition of lack. We may think we are struck
down, feeling cast down, prostrate, and thrown
down. But we are not destroyed. We are not
perishing. We do not die of ruin and destruction!
We are not lost and experiencing a miserable
end!"

This was Paul's identity; he knew who he was in Christ. In
asking God to remove a thorn, he had a momentary tempta-
tion to believe a lie that he was lacking something in Christ.

Verse 7 says that the treasure we have in our physical bodies (our jars
of clay) is the Light! Our identity is His life IN us, AS us! Paul lived
his life by the faith OF the Son of God. He believed what the Son of
God believes. He agreed with God in ALL things. We have the faith

of God IN us; His faith is our faith. And when we agree with Him, we effortlessly believe what He believes.

God's faith sees reality from the unseen realm. It goes beyond physical sight or what we can see with our natural eyes. 2 Kings 6:14–17 tells the story of Elisha's servant Gehazi. He could only see the enemies surrounding them in the natural realm and asked Elisha, "What shall we do?" Elisha told him not to be afraid and prayed for God to open Gehazi's eyes to see the unseen realm all around them, to see their victory!

Gehazi didn't have an enemy problem; he had a sight or perception problem.

Once his eyes were opened, he saw what was real before him— complete victory! Gehazi's name means the valley of sight or vision. We aren't to perceive things from the valley, from the lower realm. We are co-seated in Him, and we are to see and understand things from that vantage point. From that vantage point, we can only see complete victory! There are no advancing enemies of sin, death, satan, sickness, disease, poverty, etc. All died two thousand years ago! God's faith only sees complete victory! Gehazi's eyes were opened to see what was always real and all around him, even when he couldn't see it with his natural vision.

The victory was always there, and it was more real than anything he could see in the natural, sense realm.

God's faith sees *and* speaks.

Hebrews 11:3 says, *"Faith understands that the spoken word* (the rhema) *of God formed the universe so that what is seen was not made out of what was visible."*

The root of the Greek word for 'formed' means "at the present time," or "right NOW!" God's faith understands that the spoken word has the power to create our world right now. We don't have to strive to get enough faith or build up our faith to form our world. No! We have God's faith IN us. Mark 11:22 doesn't tell us to have faith in God. It tells us to have God's faith. The Greek word 'have' is echo, meaning to hold, to resonate; to echo. We are to echo God's faith. Verses 23 and 24 tell us what God's faith looks like: it believes and speaks. We are to echo what God (Father, Son, and Spirit) believes and speaks.

Earlier in the chapter, we looked in-depth at 2 Corinthians 4:8–9, where Paul tells us what it looks like when going through intense persecutions or troubles. And in verses 10–12, he continues, "Always carrying about in the body the dying of the Lord Jesus, that the life of Jesus also may be manifested in our body. 11 For we who live are always delivered to death for Jesus' sake, that the life of Jesus also may be manifested in our mortal flesh. 12 So then death is working in us, but life in you." Paul says that wherever he goes, and whatever he encounters in his body because of persecution, he knows and understands that he co-died with Jesus. And that knowing confirms that he also right now co-lives with Him because he co-resurrected with Him.

I love verses 11–12 in the Mirror Bible. It says, "Our
day-to-day experience continues to exhibit that
even in the face of death, our association with the
death Jesus already died remains the inspiration
of His life made so clearly visible within us. This
is in such contrast to the circumstances that we
are often faced with. 12 Our persuasion of our
co-crucifixion with Christ in the face of death-
threatening circumstances inspires life in you!"

And then Paul says in verse 13, "And since we have the same spirit of
faith, according to what is written, 'I believed and therefore I spoke,'
we also believe and therefore speak."

Here, Paul quotes David in Psalm 116. David was at a low place in
his life. In verses 3–4, he says that the pains of death surrounded him.
It says that the territory or region of death surrounded him. In other
words, all he could see was death all around him. He went on to say
that the grave had found him; trouble and sorrow were all David had
found. BUT the Lord saved him! So, David speaks to his soul, to his
heart, and his mind to return to their rest because he realized that
God had dealt bountifully with him. He had been good to him and
treated him well. And because of that, David said I believe, and so I
speak. Paul quoting David in 2 Corinthians 4:13, says, "We having or
echoing the same spirit of faith... we believe therefore we also speak."
The Mirror Bible says, "Our persuasion is our conversation."

Our persuasion of FINISHED is our conversation to ourselves, to others, to our world, and with Abba.

Like David, Paul was going through troubles, being intensely persecuted to the point of death. The difference between David and Paul, though, is that David said that he will call upon the Lord for deliverance in the time of these troubles. But unlike David, Paul knew we have already been delivered from death. Death is not our region or territory! It doesn't surround us.

Romans 6 says that Jesus defeated death and it no longer has dominion over us. Death is FINISHED! We believe; therefore, we speak.

The word 'therefore' is dio in Greek. It speaks of two directions expressed by looking backward to the because—and then looking forward with the therefore.

When we look backward two thousand years ago to what Jesus FINISHED for us, and as us, then we are able to properly, victoriously look forward! And then we speak that FINISHED victory forth!

Romans 10:8 tells us that the rhema of faith or the spoken word of faith is near you; it is at hand. It is ready! Where is it? He goes on to say that it is in your mouth and in your heart! Just open your mouth and speak what your heart knows is true. What it is persuaded of. What it co-believes with God (Father, Son, and Spirit).

Verse 8 in the Mirror Bible is excellent! It says, *"Right-eousness announced by God's faith is the authentic conversa-tion! Here, every definition of distance in time, space, or even indifference and hostility, is canceled. The word is no longer a distant prophetic pointer in the mouths of Moses and Elijah! They announced its destiny to be mirrored in the incarnation! 'The Word is extremely close to you. It spills over from your heart and becomes dynamic conversation in your mouth.' We publicly announce this message since we are convinced that it belongs to everyone."*

And verse 9 says, *"Now your salvation is realized! Your own words echo God's voice. The unveiling of the masterful act of Jesus forms the words in your mouth, inspired by the convic-tion in your heart that God indeed raised him from the dead."*

And then wow, verse 10! *"This is where believing happens spontaneously, in the heart! The revelation of mankind's redeemed righteousness ignites a new conversation, announcing salvation."*

And I love verse 7a in the Mirror Bible. It says, "Faith-conversation understands the resurrection-revelation (and mankind's co-inclusion in it! Hosea 6:2)." The faith conversation that flows out of our hearts

—out of our thoughts and feelings—is the language of our co-resurrection IN Christ!

God's faith speaks the language of righteousness!

t understands and speaks of FINISHED salvation (sozo—WHOLENESS!) and echoes the language of CO! Co-crucified and co-resurrected. It doesn't believe or speak thorn language. It doesn't think or speak the language of sin, death, sickness, disease, etc. It also doesn't speak the language of valley sight or low sense realm perception as Gehazi had. He has opened our eyes to see only victory! To see only FINISHED and NOW.

Jesus said in Luke 6:45 that our hearts are storehouses. They hold the treasure, and out of the heart's abundance, our mouth speaks and brings forth the treasure that is in us.

The word 'bring forth' is *prophero*, meaning to move something to necessary manifestation!

We believe, therefore we speak, and healing is manifested! We believe and speak, and prosperity is manifested! ALL the benefits of our salvation are manifested by our believing and speaking. And our believing is a co-believing... we live our life BY the faith OF the Son of God.

Our speaking is the outflow of God's faith IN us... and ALL that is IN us will manifest.

Proverbs 18:21 tells us that death and life are in the power of the tongue. One meaning of the word 'power' is border. Death and life are within the borders of the tongue. They are in the borders of our words. A border is a boundary. And our border, our boundary is IT IS FINISHED! Healing, prosperity, deliverance, wholeness in every area of our life is ALL within that boundary or limitation of FINISHED! Which really makes that border of FINISHED borderless or limitless! And our words bring what He FINISHED into manifestation.

> Philemon 1:6 says, "*Faith is made effective* (active
>   and productive) *by the acknowledgment of every
>   good thing IN us IN Christ.*"

> The word 'acknowledgment' is two words: *epi* meaning continual influence upon, and *ginosis* meaning intimate first-hand knowledge. *Epiginosis* means to become fully acquainted with.

The Greek says, "... in the acknowledgment of all good" instead of every good thing. Our faith, God's faith in us, is active and productive (producing what we speak) through our becoming fully acquainted with the ALL GOOD that is in us, IN Christ! And when we become fully acquainted with the ALL GOOD, with the FINISHED that is in us, our hearts effortlessly believe.

Then our mouths overflow with the language of ALL GOOD and FINISHED, and thorn language simply vanishes away.

---

2 Peter 1:3 tells us that *"He has given us ALL things that pertain to life and godliness."*

Ephesians 1:3 says that *"He has blessed us IN ALL spiritual blessing IN Christ."*

And 1 Timothy 6:17 says that *"God has provided us ALL things richly for our FULL enjoyment."*

So why aren't we enjoying the ALL GOOD that is in us IN Christ?

Hosea 4:6 says, "My people are destroyed for lack of knowledge." The word 'destroyed' at its root is to be silent. Lack of knowledge or lack of being fully acquainted with who we are and what we have in Christ causes us to be silent. But Matthew 10:27 says, "What you hear in your ear, you will shout from the rooftops!" The word 'ear' means the faculty of perception. And the good news is that He has forever freed us to hear what He hears and speaks in us.

Knowing the ALL GOOD in us IN CHRIST causes our mouth to overflow with those good things. And our faith (His faith in us) becomes effective, calling those things that are not into existence and framing your world!

> We're not talking about religious formulas, discipline, or willpower

> We're not talking about if we can just "believe" enough or "confess" enough.

Calling those things that are not into existence and framing our worlds flows out of the understanding, the revelation, of our FINISHED identity as heirs of salvation and co-heirs with Christ Jesus. Confession is simply agreeing with God and saying what He says. Agreeing with Him that yes, we are an heir of salvation, and ALL that salvation provides is mine NOW! And out of that agreement or believing, our hearts overflow with praise. Praise is acknowledgment and means to tell the story. And the thing about praise is that it has a hard time remaining silent!

A FINISHED salvation is our inheritance—deliverance, prosperity, healing, and wholeness in ALL areas of our lives are ours to FULLY enjoy NOW in this life.

Become thoroughly acquainted with your inheritance and shout it from the rooftops! IT IS FINISHED!

Chapter 16

War No More!

M ost believers in the church are passionate about being "soldiers for Christ" and diligent in warfare. I was one of them. But I let that go a few years ago and haven't looked back. As a result, I have experienced such beautiful freedom—freedom from fear and from striving. However, I am not writing this chapter to tell you what to believe regarding spiritual warfare. I simply want to challenge you to make your understanding of IT IS FINISHED bigger than it is right now. As it gets bigger, what you currently believe about warfare will change.

Peter said in 2 Peter 3:18 that we are to grow or increase in grace and knowledge of our Lord and Savior Jesus Christ! We should continually be growing in what we know to be true about Jesus and what He FINISHED for us and *as us*.

In previous chapters, we looked at the word FINISHED or *tetelestai* in Greek and saw that it was a loud battle cry to lay your weapons down and go home because the war was over. It was the loud declaration that the enemy had been completely defeated. It was a final and full victory! Warfare can only take place between two *undefeated* foes. But once an enemy has been conquered, the war is over, and there is peace. Jesus conquered all enemies—the war is over.

Let's dive deeper into this truth and explore the freedom and peace that come from embracing the reality of Christ's COMPLETE victory.

> It is FINISHED... such beautiful, complete, and final
> words of our victory in Christ. Abba said similar
> words in Genesis when He declared, "It is VERY
> GOOD," or in Hebrew, "*TOV MEOD!*"

Tov meod is to declare something is the best of the best of the best... *and better than the absolute best of the best!*

The word *tov* in Hebrew means good, beautiful, and working the way it was designed to function. It is a word meaning whole and complete. The root of the word is *tet-bet* and means to prepare something to receive. The ancient root of *tov* is the house surrounded by grace, beauty, love, health, and prosperity.

We are His house, created for a life of grace, beauty, love, and prosperity. He prepared this earth to be good, beautiful, prosperous, and functioning perfectly. He created it complete and whole. He prepared it FINISHED for His beloved children. Adam and Eve were to simply rest in it and enjoy the grace, beauty, love, and prosperity that Abba had prepared for them.

David is an example of a father who also prepared something very good and complete for his son to rest in. He, as a type of Christ, establishes his kingdom by prevailing over all enemies. He prepared a victorious kingdom for his son, Solomon, to receive. Solomon's reign was peaceful and quiet from enemies (SEE 1 CHRONICLE 22:9). It was an undisturbed kingdom. He had rest from his enemies on every side with not a single enemy to contend with. Absolute peace surrounded him

---

The word 'peace' is *shalom*, meaning favor, good health, prosperity, completeness. The root of the word is shalem, which means finished, complete, and safe in body, mind, and estate. It signifies being completed, restored, and made whole!

Peace and quiet entirely surrounded Solomon! The word 'quiet' is *shaqat* and means to be undisturbed, still, at rest! Undisturbed rest surrounded Solomon! This was Solomon's kingdom to be enjoyed. There was no battle or warfare needed. He was simply able to enjoy and delight in everything his father had lovingly prepared for him. It was a dominion of rest—a FINISHED kingdom with absolutely no threat of enemies.

Jesus gave us a FINISHED kingdom to enjoy with no threat of enemies. Yet, as Christians, we've become overly demon—or enemy— conscious. Believing an enemy attacks us when we are out of the will of God. And also believing that he attacks us when we are in the will of God and need to be stopped from advancing the kingdom. Both beliefs produce either condemnation or self-righteousness in our thinking.

> But our life is not lived on a battlefield. Our life is a
> kingdom of VICTORY! The battle has already
> been won! FINISHED!

Instead of being demon or devil-conscious and warfare focused, we need to be FINISHED conscious! Victory conscious! Because the enemy was 100% COMPLETELY defeated, stripped, and rendered powerless two thousand years ago!

Unfortunately, some of these ancient pagan beliefs mirror what we believe in Christianity today. Israel absorbed the religious beliefs of the surrounding nations, blending them with their faith in God. For instance, Numbers 25:3 says Israel yoked herself to Baal-peor, a Canaanite god.

The pagan nations of the Old Testament were highly demon and devil-conscious. Defense against evil spirits was a major concern for them. They considered demons as evil gods with different classes and levels, and believed that sickness came from demonic possession. For example, they had specific demons for specific ailments, like a headache demon or fever demon. Canaanite demonology even depicted a demon with two horns and a tail, and much of their magic focused on protecting against or expelling demons.

Israel, during their times of captivity, absorbed and mixed these pagan religious beliefs with their belief in God. Numbers 25:3 says that Israel yoked herself to Baal-peor, a Canaanite god. The Israelites believed that demons lived in deserts or ruins, inflicted sickness, troubled minds, and deceived people. Unlike the pagans, however, they believed God sent these demons or evil spirits. This co-mingling of beliefs led to a distorted understanding of God and His nature.

So, why so much warfare in the body of Christ if the enemy was defeated and stripped of all power two thousand years ago?

Because we've been taught to believe that we have an enemy named Satan who opposes God, and therefore opposes us and is continually attacking us. But in the Hebrew Bible, the word "satan" was never used as a proper name. It was merely a term used to identify an adversary. In early Hebrew traditions, there was no "Satan" with a capital S, no devil, demons, or hell. Early Judaism didn't believe in Satan as Christians do. They described satan as one who works for God, a messenger doing the Lord's bidding as an adversary. It is not a prince of darkness but a flesh-and-blood human opponent or an angel of the Lord, as in Numbers 22. However, by the time the book of Job was written, early in the Second Temple period (around 2,500 years ago), satan was developing into an evil being.

It's only in the English Bibles where satan is written with a capital S. In the Hebrew Bibles, it is *ha'satan* or the adversary. In Job and Zechariah, *ha'satan* or the adversary is described as a member of God's heavenly court, a kind of prosecutor.

The one and only time in the Hebrew Bible that satan is used as a proper name is in the Book of Chronicles. He appears in revisions of the books of Samuel, Kings, and the Book of Chronicles, probably dated to the late 4th or early 3rd century B.C. This was the period when the Hebrew Bible was translated into Greek, and the word used for the noun satan was *diabolos*, meaning one who slanders or accuses. The English Bibles translated this word diabolos as Devil (with a capital D). This was also when the books of the Watchers, Enoch, Jubilees, etc., were written. They were not part of the canon of the Bible, but they were popular at the time. These books contain hordes of evil demons and a chief leader or demon who oppose God and oversee a group of fallen angels who spread evil throughout the world.

How did the Jews of that era come up with the idea of a chief demon responsible for evil?

One rabbi explains, *"The ancient world struggled with the coexistence of good and evil, and so they hypothesized a kind of demonic, divine force that was responsible for evil, arising out of the notion that a good god could not be responsible for bad things."*

But they didn't come up with this idea all on their own. They absorbed and mingled the beliefs of the ancient, pagan nations around them with their own belief in God, leading to a warped, distorted view of God and the world. In this case, they adopted ideas from their Persian captors, who ruled over the entire Middle East from 539 to 330 B.C.

The Persian religion, Zoroastrianism, envisioned the universe as a battleground between two opposing supreme gods: Ahura Mazda, the "wise lord," and Angra Mainyu, the "destructive spirit."

Zoroastrianism influenced both Judaism and Christianity and continues to shape our beliefs today. In our Christian Bibles, the Hebrew word satan evolved into the Antichrist — God's antithesis, who is behind all evil and is the master of hell. English translations of the Bible began capitalizing the S in satan and the D in devil, making them proper nouns, as if referring to an evil entity. However, in Greek, the word devil is diabolos and isn't used as a proper noun. It's not even a noun but rather an adjective. In the Septuagint, it is used for verses about satan, such as in Job. It means slandering or accusing, not *the* Slanderer or *the* Accuser. The exception is three different occasions where it talks about human behavior and calls the person a false accuser (noun). But nowhere in Scripture does it refer to a demonic entity called the Devil. Even in Ephesians 6, where translations say, "the fiery darts of the evil one," it isn't a noun either. The "evil one" is an adjective describing the darts... *evil darts*.

Devil or *diabolos* comes from a compound word. *Dia* means because or through, and *ballo*, meaning to cast down.

It is referring to the cast-down condition mankind suffered in because of Adam's fall. It was the fallen mindset of humanity.

Why is all this important?

Because if we don't understand where these concepts and ideas came from, we will think they are true, believing they came from God when in reality, they are men's own distorted thoughts.

These pagan nations of the Old Testament believed in evil spirits, and Israel adopted the belief that these evil spirits were sent by God.

But what does the Bible say about spirits?

In Genesis, the word "spirit" referred to the Spirit of God, the life or spirit of man, and the soul's emotions. Genesis 2:7 states, "And the LORD God formed the man out of the dust of the ground and breathed the breath of life into his nostrils, and the man became a living being." This breath of life from God made man a living being, or "chayah nephesh" in Hebrew, which means a soul alive. The term "nephesh" encompasses soul, life, personhood, desires, appetites, and emotions—essentially, our inner being made up of spirit and soul (mind, will, emotions, and conscience).

Throughout Genesis, whenever spirit is mentioned, it refers to God's spirit or man's spirit and soul. Occasionally, it refers to the wind. When speaking of God's Spirit, it is associated with creation (Genesis 1:2), intimate fellowship with mankind (Genesis 3:8), and the breath of life in His creation (Genesis 7:15, 22).

The first time "spirit" is connected with man, it refers to his mind and emotions.

For example, in Genesis 26:35, Isaac and Rebekah's minds were grieved or bitter because of Esau's foreign wives. This grief of mind was an emotion of the soul, not a "spirit of grief."

In Genesis 41:8, Pharaoh's spirit was troubled, leading him to call for magicians, astrologers, and wise men of Egypt to address his anxiety. This troubled spirit was an emotion of his soul. In a pagan nation like

Egypt, the cure for these soul emotions (translated as spirit) was to call on magicians and sorcerers.

Exodus 6:9 mentions that the children of Israel wouldn't listen to Moses because of a "broken spirit." Their spirit was broken due to the cruelty and bondage of slavery, resulting in feelings of discouragement and despondency. This broken spirit interfered with their ability to hear and respond to God's promise of deliverance. Their prolonged exposure to harsh labor and a pagan culture that worshipped over 2,000 gods had affected their inner being, leading to despair and hopelessness. It affected their spirit which was their soul emotions.

In Numbers 5:14, we encounter another mention of the word "spirit." Unlike earlier references where it described soul emotions, it now refers to a "spirit OF something." It says that a "spirit of jealousy" came upon a husband, leading him to accuse his wife of adultery. He would then take her to the priest, who made her drink bitter water mixed with ink and ash. If her belly swelled and her thigh rotted, she was deemed guilty of adultery. Seriously?!

All of this is presented as Yahweh, or I AM, instructing Moses in verse 11. Personally, I think Moses brought these ideas from his life in Egypt.

In Egypt, rivers and waters were believed to have magical powers, and adulterous women were thrown into them. If they drowned, they were guilty. What an incredible, crazy idea! So, we have to read this account in Numbers 5 and conclude that NO, this was NOT the Lord saying this; it had to be Moses!

Those verses in Numbers 5 are filled with *aleph tavs*. In our English Bibles, it is untranslatable, and in Hebrew grammar, they serve as direct object markers. I believe it is a direct object marker in the sense that they directly point to Jesus as the object of verses—in other words, He is our lens of interpretation.

Aleph and *tav* are the first and last letters of the Hebrew alphabet, just like the Greek letters *alpha* and *omega* are the first and last letters of the Greek Alphabet. Jesus is the *Aleph* and the *Tav*, the *Alpha* and *Omega,* the *Beginning* and the *End.*

The rabbis interpret it as the first matter out of which all things were formed.

In ancient Hebraic word pictures, *aleph tav* is strength and cross—the strength or power of the cross. It's like a marker or a signpost in a verse where God is saying, "STOP! I put the *aleph tav* (the mark of the power of the cross) here so that you will remember to read this through the lens of the FINISHED work of Christ."

These prophetic pointers (**את**) sprinkled through
these verses are saying, "Hey... look at Jesus! He's
the only One who intimately knows the Father!

The verses we are reading in Numbers 5 do not reflect the nature of
Abba that Jesus revealed. Jesus revealed to us how Abba deals with
an issue of adultery.

In the Gospels, a woman caught in adultery is brought and thrown
before Jesus. He didn't demand that she be thrown in a river or be
commanded to drink ink and ash water. NO! He revealed the
Father's heart toward her—compassionate mercy and unconditional
love! Grace was extended to her!

Acts 7:22 says that Moses was instructed with *all* the wisdom
of Egypt. All means ALL! Part of his instruction in the
wisdom of Egypt would've included training in the magic arts,
and perhaps some of it was still a part of his thinking.

Paul didn't call jealousy a spirit. He called jealousy, *as well as
adultery*, a work of the flesh in Galatians 5. He also called witchcraft
and idolatry a work of the flesh. This prescription for determining the
woman's guilt or innocence in Numbers 5 was definitely witchcraft
which is merely a work of the flesh!

So, you can see that man's spirit is affected by his mind (thoughts) and emotions. It's understandable that 400 years of bondage to a pagan nation could cause the Israelites to believe in spirits OF this or that, making them entities. The cures for these spirits resembled the magic practiced in these pagan religions—practices that we could call witchcraft or, as Paul called it, a work of the flesh—not a demonic spirit!

It's easy to see that some of our beliefs in modern Christianity about spiritual warfare and demonology are rooted in the pagan religious beliefs of ancient Mesopotamia and Egypt.

We say that we believe Jesus defeated the enemy. But our need to enforce that victory through constant warfare shows that we don't believe it was a completely FINISHED defeat.

But how FINISHED is FINISHED when it comes to spiritual warfare?

Isaiah 40:2 declares, "Speak kindly to Jerusalem; And call out to her, that her warfare has ended, that her iniquity has been removed, that she has received of the LORD'S hand double for all her sins." This passage literally means to speak to Jerusalem's heart. Jerusalem, the dwelling place of God, represents us—the NEW Jerusalem. What message was to be spoken to Jerusalem's heart, to her thoughts and feelings? **Her warfare has ended!**

The word 'warfare' is *tsaba*, meaning warfare, army, and battle. The root means to wage war. The word 'ended' is *mala*, meaning fulfilled; completed; FINISHED!

The phrase "double for all her sins" doesn't mean that God punished Jerusalem double for her sins. It refers to an Eastern custom: if a man owed a debt he couldn't pay, his creditor would write the amount on paper and nail it to the man's front door for everyone to see. But if someone paid the debt, the creditor would double the paper over and nail it to the door as a testimony that the debt was fully paid.

This is a beautiful picture in Isaiah 40, announcing to Israel that in the death and resurrection of their Messiah, the debt they *thought* they owed has been fully paid. Their warfare was over, all "assumed" debts were paid, and they were free to live in peace and security!

Warfare, armies, battles, and waging is completely unnecessary! We reign in peace. We reign in a FINISHED, undisturbed kingdom of rest.

There was a real enemy against man. Genesis 3 tells us that the serpent deceived Eve. She believed the false accusation that she wasn't like God. Paul wrote about it in 2 Corinthians 11:3, saying, "But I fear, lest by any means, as the serpent beguiled Eve through his subtilty, so your minds should be corrupted from the simplicity that is in Christ." Eve was seduced and thoroughly deceived. Her mind became corrupted because she believed a lie about herself.

She and Adam believed the lie that they were not entirely made in the image of God. Embracing that lie—a false perception of themselves—changed their perception of God. They no longer saw God as He truly was, a loving Father passionate about them. This false perception made them think they were separated from God. Colossians 1:21 says, "And you, that were once alienated and enemies in your mind by wicked works, yet now has he reconciled."'"

The idea that they were alienated and enemies of God was in their minds only.

There are different words in the New Testament to describe this enemy—satan, devil, adversary, thief, etc. I encourage you to look them up and read them in context to understand what the writers are referring to, rather than automatically assuming they refer to a demonic agent against you that you need to battle. For instance, the thief in John 10:10 is called the enemy but refers to the Pharisees' false teachings, not a devil or satan!

Re-read the verses you believe are about warfare in context, consider who the writer is talking to and interpret them through the lens of it is FINISHED.

Take 1 Timothy 6:12, for example, where Paul tells Timothy to fight the good fight of faith. In context, 1 Timothy is talking about false teachings that were circulating.

The word 'fight' refers to a struggle in the soul (mind, will, and emotions). It is derived from the root word *ago*.

I got excited when I saw that the root word for fight is *ago*! It's one of my favorite words.

Right there in the root meaning of the word fight (or struggling in the soul) is the answer to how to fight. This root word *ago* means to lead in Greek.

It is equivalent to the Hebrew word *nachal*, which also means to lead *and* rest. The more literal meaning of the word is a combination of both these ideas. It is to lead one to a place of rest.

Christ has already fought and won the fight for us, and as us! He has already led us to a place of rest... *co-seated with Him.* You don't need to do warfare because *in Him,* you have already won the battle.

His victory is already YOUR victory! There is no enemy to fight. This is simply a call to rest in what He FINISHED!

As we begin to understand that it is FINISHED and recognize that He has led us to a position of rest, these soul struggles (in our minds, will, and emotions) will cease to be a struggle. We will realize that He has brought us to a place of rest where nothing more is required of us. Our testimony is always it is FINISHED! 2 Corinthians 2:14 says, "Thanks be to God who *always*, and *at all times*, leads us in triumph."

Leading in triumph means publicly exalting the victor who leads the victory procession and putting the conquered enemy on display— exhibiting him as totally defeated. We are the victors! We lead the victory procession, publicly revealing the enemy as COMPLETELY DEFEATED. No warfare is necessary because the enemy is already defeated.

And FINISHED means exactly that—FINISHED!

The enemy was conquered, not just confronted and rebuked. The only power the enemy has now is through deception and lies. But understand, it's an imaginary power, not a real one. It's not a power of any substance—it only exists in the imaginations and minds of those who don't fully understand the FINISHED work of Jesus Christ and their identity in Him.

If you still think you need to engage in spiritual warfare against an enemy's attacks, consider these verses in Isaiah.

Isaiah 35:8–9 describes our new life in Christ as an eternal highway of holiness. And verse 9 says, *"No lion shall be* (exist, arise, appear, continue) *there, nor any ravenous beast shall go up* (reach, invade) *there on, it shall not be found* (be able, come forth, appear, take hold) *there; but the redeemed shall walk there."*

The word 'ravenous' is parits in Hebrew, meaning violent, vicious, robbers (thieves), and destroyers. The root means to break through.

Colossians 3 tells us that our life is hidden with Christ in God. Being hidden in God means that no ravenous beast, no enemy, can break through or invade our life. Nothing is invading Jesus, and as He is so are we; therefore, nothing invades us either! This place of understanding is the highway of holiness that Isaiah talked about—a high place where no enemy, nothing unclean, and no ravenous beast will be found. We were raised with Him, in Him, and are co-seated far above all powers and principalities in this world. Living in a time and space earth life that is engaged in eternal now throne room thinking.

It is an awareness of the spirit realm that is more real than the natural, earthly realm we walk in.

There is no lion or ravenous beast on this highway... *there is no enemy to be found!* Nor shall any enemy go up on it. Highways in the Old Testament were designed for ease of travel, unhindered because ALL obstacles have been removed. A highway is a road built up and raised above its surroundings. And this highway is for the redeemed.

It is an understanding of all humanity raised up in Christ—an awareness of our co-seated-ness in Him.

The ancient root of the word redeemed means dancing in a circle. It's the picture of this beautiful eternal dance of oneness... of Father, Son, Spirit, and ALL humanity dancing together!

Twirling about in Divine union. They in us and us in Them... *living, laughing, and loving undisturbed as one!*

So, as we go higher in our thinking, we realize we are truly hidden with Christ in God. This is our dwelling place. To dwell in Hebrew means to sit down. It is a position of rest.

This place of rest is where we realize there is no enemy to battle because Jesus defeated ALL enemies.

It's not a high place where the enemy is not allowed to touch us. It's the high place where we realize there is no enemy! From God's perspective, he no longer exists because he was totally, completely destroyed! And it's not the high place where we must use our faith to get there. It's the high place where we realize it's where we have always been. And because it's FINISHED, we can't be unseated.

Ephesians 2:6 says that we are co-seated with Him in heavenly places. We died with Him, were buried with Him, resurrected with Him, ascended with Him, and we were seated with Him. None of it was our doing; it was all Him. All of those are aorist indicative—past tense facts! FINISHED! And, they are in the active voice, which means the subject of the sentence is performing the action. The subject of the sentence is Jesus. He raised you up, and He seated you in the heavenly realms, with Him, and in Him. All that is needed is to simply change our thinking.

Paul in 1 Timothy 1:18 describes what good warfare or ideal warfare looks like.

It says, "*This charge I entrust to you, Timothy, my child, in accordance with the prophecies previously made about you, that by them you may wage the good warfare...*"

And verse 19 says, "*holding faith and a good conscience.*"

Whose faith are we holding? His faith. It's always about His faith in us! Galatians 2:20: "this life I now live, I live BY THE FAITH OF THE SON OF GOD." Understanding that it is His faith in us takes the pressure off us to have great faith or try to increase our faith. It's

His faith in us... just like it's *His* strength, *His* peace, *His* wisdom, etc.... it's *His* faith! So, we hold *His* faith in us, and that's the faith we live by. And then it says and a good conscience.

The word 'conscience' is *suneidesis*, which is two words: *sun*, meaning together with, and *eido*, meaning to see and know. It is a co-knowing and a co-seeing.

We hold or echo His faith, co-knowing, and co-seeing with Him, from where we are co-seated with Him. It goes on to say *in accordance with the prophecies*. Revelation 19:10 says that the testimony of Jesus is the spirit of prophecy.

What is the testimony of Jesus? **IT IS FINISHED!**

Paul is telling Timothy (and us) that the good warfare we wage regarding the prophecies that were made about us is the report of the FINISHED work of Jesus. It is resting in His faith and co-knowing and co-seeing with Him.

In Exodus 14:13 it says, *"And Moses said unto the people, 'Fear ye not, stand still, and see the salvation of the LORD, which he will shew to you*

today: for the Egyptians whom ye have seen today,
ye shall see them again no more forever.'"

Here we see a picture of the children of Israel being delivered out of bondage. Their enemy (the Egyptians — a type of death) was COMPLETELY defeated. Never to be seen again.

The word 'see' in Hebrew is *raah*, meaning to see, experience, perceive, and think. 1 Corinthians 2:16 says we have the mind of Christ. The Amplified version says we hold His thoughts, purposes, and intents of His heart.

Our minds are not a battlefield—we have HIS mind.

And as we believe that, our minds will begin to reflect His thoughts, purposes, and intents of His heart. And our minds will be thinking FINISHED thoughts. We have been given an *eternally* secure victory.

Hebrews 2:6–8 says, "*What is man, that thou art*
    mindful of him? Or the son of man, that thou
    visitest him? [7] Thou madest him a little lower than
    the angels; thou crownest him with glory and honor,
    and didst set him over the works of thy hands: [8]
    Thou hast put all things in subjection under his

feet. For in that he put all in subjection under him,
he left nothing that is not put under him. But now
we see not yet all things put under him."

Sometimes in life, it doesn't seem like we walk in the victory that is ours. It doesn't look like everything is always under our feet. However, verse 9 says, "but we see Jesus!" The word 'see' in Greek is *blepo*, meaning to observe and watch carefully.

By observing Him, seeing Him as He is — we see ourselves!

Jesus not only destroyed the enemy. He also destroyed the *works* of the enemy. 1 John 3:8 says, "For this reason, the Son of God was revealed, that He might destroy the works of the devil." The word 'devil' here isn't a noun but an adjective. It is a word describing the noun. It is *diabolos* and means through falling or through being cast down. It has to do with accusation.

The fall came through the accusation that Adam and Eve were not already just like God. That is what is being said through the Greek word devil. It is not a demonic entity with two horns, a tail, and a pitchfork! It's the accusation of the lie that we are not already like God.

The word 'works' is *erga* in Greek, meaning tasks, actions, a deed, or activity carried out, behaviors, labors, business. It means *doing*.

There is nothing this devil can do to us because Jesus completely destroyed *all* the devil's works—*all* the accusations, behaviors, labors, experiences, *all* the doings that came out of the fallen mindset, the sacrificial system, etc.

For those still having a difficult time letting go of the idea you've had of satan or the devil, that's ok. You can continue to have your understanding of who or what the enemy is. But what is important is knowing that **Jesus COMPLETELY DESTROYED ALL HIS WORKS!** He can't attack you. And he can't lie to you, deceive you, lead you astray, plot against you, inflict disease/sickness, or cause division in your life. He can't do anything! Why not? Because ALL his "doing" was completely destroyed!

What does a chapter on warfare as a FINISHED work have to do with a book on healing?

Everything!

Because if we think we still have an enemy that we must war against or a mind that is a battleground, then we won't realize that we are whole and complete. That we were healed two thousand years ago! We will always see sickness and disease as an attack by an unseen enemy, and we will see health as something we can lose. But IT IS FINISHED! The I AM is healed and whole, so, therefore, we are healed and whole! Because as He is, so are we in this world!

The key is waking up to who we already are: sons, victors, ruling, and reigning from a seated position of rest—a FINISHED position of complete victory.

John says in 1 Jn 4:17, *"As He is, so are we in this world!"*

He is seated. He is not still arming Himself against a defeated enemy. And we are seated with Him. So why are we still arming ourselves against an enemy who was 100% defeated two thousand years ago?

We are co-seated VICTORS. We reign in an undisturbed kingdom of peace. ALL warfare is 100% FINISHED. Abba is speaking tenderly to our hearts, "Your warfare has ended! Enter into My rest."

Chapter 17

The Minister of Our Tabernacle

A few years ago, everything clicked for me regarding divine health and wholeness after I listened to a revelatory teaching by Mike Miller on Jesus being the Minister of our tabernacle. In that moment, everything fell into place, and my understanding of living a life of divine health became effortless and clear. The revelation of what Jesus FINISHED for the health of our bodies exploded within me, and I was never the same again. There was no more back-and-forth in my thinking. This revelation marked a profound transformation in my life, dividing it into two distinct phases: who I was before and who I am now—FREE!

Unfortunately, much of our understanding of healing comes from an Old Covenant perspective we glean from the gospels. But we need to move beyond that. We need to reach a place where we can effortlessly and fearlessly experience ALL that Jesus FINISHED for us and as us. We need a New Covenant understanding, not merely of healing, but of our restored divine health and wholeness.

Hebrews 8:2 says, *"A minister of the sanctuary, and of the true tabernacle, which the Lord pitched, and not man."*

The sanctuary refers to our innermost being. It is the holy place and represents our spirit and soul. The tabernacle is our physical body. Hebrews 8:1 says the main point or the FINALITY of everything is we have a High Priest who SAT DOWN!

Our seated High Priest, with whom we are co-seated, is the Minister of both our sanctuary and our tabernacle. This is the office He occupies as our High Priest. He ministers in our inner man and in our outer man.

Why was He seated? Because ALL was FINISHED!

He sat down because there is nothing more that needs to be done. ALL humanity has been 100% redeemed, 100% reconciled to God, and 100% delivered from all the effects of the curse that had come upon man as a result of sin. ALL sin has been canceled, death defeated, and the fall and its effects on humanity and the world no longer exist.

Mankind has been redeemed and set free to live as God originally designed: as sons created in His image and likeness with dominion over ALL the works of His hand.

However, I get asked all the time, "But Robin, how can you say that? Everything I see in the world contradicts that!" And yes, I agree. There are definitely things existing in this world today that were canceled by the FINISHED work of Jesus long ago.

So, how is this possible? It comes down to the power of belief.

In ALL of us is the creative likeness of God. Although sin, sickness, disease, death, and everything resulting from the fall were canceled and rendered powerless, our belief in their continued existence can resurrect them in our personal experiences.

Our thoughts and words can breathe life back into what was meant to be dead and gone. While the world may look like a contradiction to Christ's FINISHED work, YOU are the only one with the authority to revive or banish these defeated foes in your life.

---

1 Corinthians 6:19–20 says that our body is the temple of the Spirit of God *in* us. And then Paul says our body *and* our spirit are not ours but are both God's. We are not our own—our spirit is not our own, *and* our body is not our own. The word "are" in Greek is *este* meaning to exist.

Our body doesn't exist as our own. Our spirit doesn't exist as our own. They belong to God!

Paul continues, saying we are to glorify God in our spirit *and* our bodies. Glory is the manifested presence of God. In other words, we are to understand that our spirit *and* our bodies are the manifested presence of God!

Some of the synonyms for glorify are exalt, magnify, make large, honor. Paul is telling us to magnify and enlarge our understanding of who God is IN us. We are to exalt in our understanding and perception that God's manifested presence is in our spirit (our sanctuary) *and* in our body (or tabernacle).

Notice Hebrews 8:2 doesn't say Jesus is a Minister *to* our sanctuary and tabernacle but a Minister *of*. What's the difference?

He ministered **to** the sanctuary when He became sin, addressing the spiritual condition of humanity post-Adam's fall.

He ministered **to** the tabernacle when He became the curse, dealing with all the natural corruption that came with sin's distorted mindset.

The word "minister" in Hebrews 8:2 is not the commonly used *diachanos*, which refers to someone currently serving you—bringing meals, asking if you need anything else. That's not the term used here.

Jesus is not still serving or ministering to you, asking if you need anything else. He already did that. He completely ministered *to* your sanctuary and tabernacle. It is FINISHED, and now He's SEATED.

He sat down because He became sin and became the curse. ALL that is done. Now, He's the Minister *of* your sanctuary and tabernacle. The word "minister" here is *leitourgos*, meaning a functionary in the Temple. A functionary is responsible for the care and management of ALL entrusted to Him.

Jesus is entrusted with the care, maintenance, and upkeep of both our inner man and our outer man. And He's SEATED.

What does that mean? It means both your sanctuary AND your tabernacle are perfected, accomplished, and secure forever. Jesus has made Himself responsible for our wholeness, health, prosperity, and freedom in our spirit, soul, AND physical body.

He's the Functionary of our spirit, mind, will, emotions, AND physical body. He's the One appointed by the Father to oversee our *entire* being—spirit, soul, *and* body.

In other words, He ALONE is responsible for our care and maintenance. That's a place of rest for you and me!

We can cease making ourselves responsible for our healing, trying to work through formulas and keys. We can simply rest in the fact that

He is our Functionary, taking care of our entire being—spirit, soul, and body.

*So, here's what we need to understand... **the health of our physical man is just as CERTAIN as the perfection of our spirit man!***

Here's what we need to understand: the health of our physical man is just as CERTAIN as the perfection of our spirit man!

Most of us believe in the 100% perfection of our spirit. We trust that nothing can defile our spirit because Jesus lives in us, making our spirit perfect like Him. Unfortunately, we don't hold the same belief about our bodies. We think our bodies won't be made new until we get to heaven someday. Until then, we see only our spirit as 100% perfect. In other words, we believe we are only 1/3 fully redeemed right now.

But we need to have the same assurance, the same confidence, the same sense of completion and perfection regarding the health of our soul and body.

He FINISHED ALL and sat down. Now, He is responsible for the care and maintenance of our entire being—spirit, soul, and body!

He's not a servant to be summoned (a *diachanos*); He is the minister OF.

> **Romans 10:6 says,** *"But the righteousness of faith speaks in this way DO NOT SAY in your heart who will ascend into heaven, that is to bring Christ down from above."*

Paul tells us clearly: DO NOT SAY in your hearts (in your thoughts and emotions) who will bring Christ down. Yet, we often do this, especially in the area of prayer. Prayer is powerful, and the power of agreement is a good thing.

We just need to learn how to pray in agreement with what He has FINISHED for us and as us.

Too often, people pray, asking for Jesus to come and heal them. But He's already ministered to our tabernacle, to our physical bodies, by becoming the curse for us. Now, He is the Minister OF our physical bodies. He indwells us!

His indwelling Presence alters our identity. It transforms us in EVERY aspect—spirit, soul, *and* body. He didn't just alter our sanctuary—our spirit and soul—leaving our bodies to be subject to sickness and disease until we finally die and "get to heaven."

No. Paul said in Galatians 2 that he was crucified with Christ and it is no longer he who lives but Christ lives *in* him and the life he lives *in the flesh* (in his physical body) he lives from or by the faith of the Son of God. Paul lived his life in his body from Jesus' faith.

Do you think Jesus' faith is believing that we must struggle in our physical bodies until we die? No! His indwelling Life transforms our lives. His Presence in us makes us wholly transformed, perfect, and whole, spirit, soul, and body. Let's embrace that truth and pray with the full understanding of our complete, finished redemption.

Hebrews 10:5 says, "A body You have prepared for Me." Many assume that God prepared Jesus' body specifically to become a sacrifice and offering for sin, believing this was God's will. However, the writer of Hebrews tells us that sacrifices and offerings were NOT the will of God; He did not desire them.

Humanity thought God required sacrifices for atonement. But Jesus refuted that assumption when He said, "BUT You have prepared a body for me." In other words, God prepared a body for Jesus because sacrifice and offering were NOT His will.

I love the Mirror translation of verse 5: So when Jesus, the Messiah, arrives as the fulfillment of all the types and shadows, he quotes Psalm 40:6-8, and says, "In sacrifices and offerings God takes no pleasure; but you have ordained my incarnation."

Was His sacrifice necessary? ABSOLUTELY. His sacrifice was a necessity, but not for God—it was necessary for humanity.

According to verse 8, sacrifices and offerings for sin were offered according to the law. But they could not remove sin. Jesus' as the Lamb of God would take away the sin of the world by becoming the FINAL sacrifice and do away with the sacrificial system that God never desired.

Verse 10 then reveals that we were sanctified through the offering of His body once for all. We often think of the body prepared for Jesus as just the physical body born to Mary that hung on the cross. No. He was not alone on that cross. It wasn't just His physical body on that cross. We were all in Him. His death was our death. Can you see the will of God declared in and through Jesus.... "There is a body that You have prepared for Me." What was the body prepared for Him? Mankind—all of us—make up the body prepared for Him; the one new man wholly sanctified in Christ.

This is the transformative power of His sacrifice: it's not just about His physical body but about us being included in His redemptive act, making us one with Him. His life in us is our life.

We are not just identified with Him in our spirits; we are identified with Him in our physical body because He took our body into Himself as His body. When He offered His body (Hebrews 10:10),

He offered His body to be shared by ALL of mankind for the rest of eternity. He brought us into His body.

That's why He remains a Man for eternity—because He made our bodies His own. He brought our bodies into His body.

WOW! This is a game-changing revelation! He brought our bodies into His body in His resurrection. Do you see the finality in that? IF He were to ever discard His body, we would all be lost! This is why Peter says Paul's words are hard to understand. And why the disciples also said Jesus' words were hard to understand about eating His flesh and drinking His blood.

Of course, Jesus did offer up His body on the cross, and I'm so grateful for that. But we need to understand that it was not the ultimate will of God. The will of God was for the everlasting identity of humanity in Christ; His life as our life.

You never again have to wonder if you're in the will of God. His will is FINISHED and perfected IN us.

He took our bodies into Himself, and our bodies are now identified in Hebrews 8:2 as the true tabernacle—or the tabernacle of Truth. And He's the Minister or the Functionary of our tabernacle. To put it simply, He's the One responsible for the care and maintenance of

BOTH the sanctuary and the tabernacle. In other words, you might say He's just taking care of Himself!

I have a friend named Yolanda who has grabbed hold of this revelation, and when she has a pain in her body, she says, "Jesus, YOU have a pain right there, what are You going to do about it?" She understands that her body is His... He is the One responsible for the care and upkeep of it.

I know some of you may read this and be thinking, "Robin, that's out of balance!!"

But when you truly embrace the good news of the Gospel of Grace, it's 100% out of balance—it was never intended to be balanced.

The radical truth of grace is that it tips the scales completely in our favor. It shatters the idea of a balanced ledger of sins and good deeds. Instead, it proclaims a finished work, a complete victory, and an all-encompassing redemption.

We are to recognize that our spirit, soul, *and* body is His and He is responsible for its care. This revelation isn't about achieving balance; it's about living in the overflow of His finished work. It's about understanding that Jesus didn't do a partial job—He finished it all. He took on our pains, our sicknesses, our struggles, and now, as the Minister of our sanctuary *and* tabernacle, He sustains us completely.

When we grasp this truth, we step into a life free from striving, free from fear, and full of His rest and wholeness. It's time to let go of the scales and embrace the radical, unbalanced, and overwhelmingly good news of the Gospel of Grace.

Now, I'm not telling you we shouldn't take care of our bodies. I don't mean it that way. But it's not about us. We need to understand that He FINISHED all and perfected us. We don't add to or take away from the wholeness that is ours by anything we do, good or bad. He made the care and upkeep of our body His responsibility.

Ephesians 5:29 says, *"No one ever hated his own flesh but nourishes and cherishes it just as the Lord does the church."* The word 'church' is *ekklesia*. It is from *ek*, meaning source and origin, and *kaleo*, meaning called, surname, or identified by name. The *ekklesia* are those whose identity is found in Him! This is ALL mankind, not a people who gather together in a building.

Jesus nourishes us, takes care of us. And verse 30 in the Mirror Bible says, "We are his flesh and bone body; bearing His image and likeness." We give a tangible expression of Him. We can rest knowing that He took our bodies into His own body... we are ONE flesh with Him. We are bone of His bone, and flesh of His flesh. He is the One responsible for the care, upkeep, and nourishing of our physical bodies!

> ### *We are not just complete in our spirit; our entire being is perfected and complete in Him.*

We don't just have this ethereal redemption that only involves our spirit. We were FULLY redeemed and perfected two thousand years ago to live AS Him who is fully resurrected from the dead on this earth. Proverbs 4 says that His word is life and health or wholeness to our flesh. Christ is the Word in us, in our tabernacle. And He's the Minister, or the One responsible for the care and upkeep of our body. His immune system, so to speak, IS our immune system, His DNA is our DNA, and His life and blood are our life and blood. *In Him*, we live and move and have our being! And likewise, *in* us, He lives and moves and has His being. It's the Word IN us that is health and life to our flesh. Not the words of the Bible that we memorize and confess when we think we need healing.

The Word, the Logos, Jesus Christ Himself is our health and life!

Is your understanding of the all-encompassing magnitude of what He FINISHED growing bigger?

Believe me, I understand these truths are not easy to grasp, just like Peter said. Much of this is new to our understanding because we've been taught a religious perspective of our redemption. But when I need help grasping them, I write them down, mull them over, and meditate on them. I speak them in agreement even when I don't fully understand, and as Andrew Wommack says he does with new truths —I speak in tongues over it. I allow the Holy Spirit to breathe on them and unfold them in my understanding.

So, "the body You have prepared for Me" refers to the transformation of mankind from Adam to Christ.

The word 'prepared' is *katartizó* in Greek and means completed thoroughly, perfectly joined together, and in good working order. Jesus didn't need to be made in good working order—mankind did. He said, "You've PREPARED it for Me." In other words, "You've completed this body thoroughly and perfectly joined together." Right there in that definition is the inclusion of ALL mankind... perfectly joined together. What did Jesus say in John 17:21? "I in You, and them in Me..."—perfectly joined together as ONE.

We were perfectly joined together with Him in good working order. And I love the root of this word "prepared." It is viewed in terms of the present, in the here and now. In the immediate present... as in right now!

When was "right now"? Two thousand years ago! So, because we've been perfectly joined together with Him—His life as our life—we're thoroughly completed and in good working order.

What is that good working order? His divine health is our divine health; His wholeness is our wholeness. In other words, our good working, thoroughly completed, and perfect immune system in our body is designed to not accept any disease but instead withstand all disease successfully! And the good working order of our bodies is just the *effortless* function of His life within us!

And the good working order of our bodies is just the effortless function of His life within us! When we get to the place where we understand this and really grasp this co-identity with Him—His life as our life—we would not even know when things come against us. Because they would come against us and be repelled.

Peter said that we are protected by the power of God through faith. It is through His faith not ours.

The same faith that justified us has provided for our protection. Protection against what? FROM ANYTHING AND EVERY-THING! I believe we'll get to the place where once again, the body of Christ is going to walk about the earth, totally untouched by sickness, disease, and any corruption or decay of our physical bodies. Where it's not Him coming to heal—it's you as Him, a co-identity, experiencing the benefit of His perfect health that indwells you.

Hebrews 10:12 says, "But this Man, after He had offered one sacrifice for sins forever, sat down at the right hand of God."

Verse 14 says, *"For by one offering He has perfected forever those who are being sanctified."*

He sat down, because we were perfected forever. FINISHED. Don't get hung up on the words "being sanctified." Our sanctification is not progressive; both perfected and sanctified are FINISHED. The word "being" is a present participle verb tense, which describes an action as having happened simultaneously with the action of the main verb: perfected. When He perfected us, we were sanctified. This communicates a FINISHED work, and we can experience our perfection and sanctification right now.

This is not a "someday" verse, nor is it about years to come after you pass from this life. And it's not after we pass trials and testing, "becoming" more like Him. Our redemption is about our life on this earth, about our experience in the here and now. God intended for man to live an abundant life from the very beginning in a delightful, pleasant, magnificently splendid environment. That's what Eden means; it is luxury, delight, pleasantness. This was God's design for us: to live in delightful surroundings, to have pleasant experiences in life, and for our life to be abundant and full of grace.

> And in Jesus, He has *eternally* secured and perfected
> what we are to experience in the here and now.
> That's amazing!

And it's so far beyond what religion has communicated. Religion always communicates boundaries and limits to grace, to perfection, to what FINISHED looks like. There are always limitations implied as to how long we can live, how healthy we can be, how prosperous, or how free we can be. Always some limit to the grace of God. Always a limit to the love and goodness of Abba. And even in our own thinking, we encounter those supposed limits. We have not allowed ourselves to believe in the perfection that the Bible declares He FINISHED for us and as us.

This generation might not see the full expression of it. Still, if someone doesn't start teaching it, there will never be a generation that believes it again!

There was a generation that believed it. That's why we see the writer of Hebrews saying perfect or perfected repeatedly. This writer was convinced of our perfection IN Christ. He or she was convinced of the finality and the main point of Jesus being seated.

We know that He is seated because He is perfect. But we need to also understand that He seated *only* because we have been made perfect. He is seated *only* because we are seated with Him. ALL is FINISHED. ALL of Adam died at the cross. NO PART of Adam survived the cross.

We are the body Abba prepared for Him. He resurrected and became that body—ONE body joined with ALL mankind!

He gave us His name and His identity. Consequently, He ALONE is responsible for the care and the maintenance of the sanctuary, our inner man (which most of us would agree), and also the tabernacle or our physical body.

Chapter 18

Co-Identity – A Single Shared Identity

When Jesus shouted, "Tetelestai!" from the cross, it was a cry of complete, 100% victory! It was a declaration of finality. He was saying, "The old has ended, it's done, it's over!"

In Revelation 21:5–6, John heard Jesus declare from the throne: *"Behold, I make ALL things new. Write: for these words are faithful and true. It is DONE! I AM the Alpha and Omega, the Beginning and the End."*

Jesus said, "I make ALL new! IT IS DONE! ALL HAS BEEN MADE NEW! IT IS FINISHED!" This declaration is not just about a future hope but a present reality. In Christ, we are new creations. Everything and everyone changed. ALL humanity was now co-seated with Him, completely whole with nothing missing, nothing broken in our lives here and now.

The grace of God is more than a concept; it is the empowering presence of Jesus in our lives, transforming us from the inside out. This grace is vast and all-encompassing, leaving no part of our lives untouched. As we embrace our co-identity with Christ, we begin to live out the reality of being made new in every aspect of our existence.

Understanding the enormity of grace means recognizing that we are no longer defined by our past or our failures. Our identity is now entirely wrapped up in Christ's finished work. We are whole, we are complete, and we are free. This is the truth of our co-identity in Christ—He has done it all, and we get to live in the fullness of His victory. This is the life we are called to live—one of victory, wholeness, and endless grace.

And here's the incredible news: no one can limit the extent of grace in our thinking or how fully we apply IT IS FINISHED to our lives. The more expansive your understanding and application, the more it might offend those around you. But don't let that deter you!

In Matthew 16, Jesus asked His disciples, "Who do men say that I am?" They responded, "Some say John the Baptist, some say Elijah, and others say Jeremiah or one of the prophets." But Jesus pressed further, "BUT who do YOU say that I am?" Peter boldly answered, "You are the Christ, the Son of the Living God."

Peter's revelation wasn't the popular opinion of the masses. It was a revelation directly from the Father, transcending common belief. And he stood firm in what Abba revealed to him.

Why is this crucial? Because as we behold Him, seeing Him as He truly is, we discover who we are. His life defines ours. Our identity is shaped by His life IN us.

Romans 6:4 says, *"Therefore we were buried with Him through baptism into death that just as Christ was raised from the dead by the glory of the Father even so we also should walk in newness of life."*

Paul is telling us that because we were joined to Him in death, we also co-raised with Him into newness of life. His resurrection life is our new life. This is true for all of humanity, whether we are aware of it or not. We didn't co-resurrect with Him when we decided to believe and say a prayer. ALL humanity rose up out of the grave with Him two thousand years ago as one new man IN Christ, alive with His resurrection life. This is our newness of life.

We need to grasp this truth because we've been living as if we need to get healed, delivered, or set free. The reality is, we are already living in this newness of life; we just haven't fully understood what it looks like. We haven't realized that ALL humanity has been restored to our original design as sons made in the image and likeness of God.

To experience the benefits of this new life—divine health, prosperity, peace—we must understand the SINGLE IDENTITY that has been imparted to us IN CHRIST, uniting us with Christ, to live AS He is in the world.

John put it perfectly: "As He is, so are we in this world." AS He is... AS the resurrected Christ. This concept is challenging because religion has taught us that we are always striving to become like Him, always in a state of becoming. You know the saying, "What would Jesus do?" And then there's the new age philosophy that removes Jesus from the equation, claiming themselves as "Christs."

But what I'm proclaiming is neither of these ideas.

I don't believe we are becoming like Him, nor do I believe that we are Christs apart from Jesus, who is THE Christ, the Son of the Living God. When I say we have a single identity AS Christ, it is only because Jesus, the Christ, fully dwells IN us! It is because of His FINISHED work in reconciling us. He took our body into His body and resurrected with ALL humanity as ONE NEW MAN. The beauty is in the individuality of His expression in and through each of us in the world.

This is what I mean by our single identity—our co-identity WITH Him, IN Him. The single identity that we share together with Him, AS Him because His life is our life.

> Single and co sound like a contradiction. But it is a
> single identity... His. And it's 'co' because we
> would not have His identity apart from Him.

Everything Paul teaches is a revelation of this single, co-identity — our shared identity AS Christ in this newness of life that we call our Christ life! It is the revelation of the Gospel. In Galatians 3, he says that because we belong to Christ, we are Abraham's seed. Not seeds, but Seed—singular. We exist and share His identity as Christ, the Seed.

This isn't blasphemous; it's the beautiful fullness of our new life IN Him. What is true of Him is true of us.

St. Athanasius said, "Jesus became what we were so that we would become what He is." When did we become what He is? Two thousand years ago when we resurrected with Him. In Galatians 2, Paul defines his new life. He said he died with Christ and no longer lives, but Christ lives IN him. Our new life is defined by union, by our ONENESS with Christ. We are the full embodiment of Him on the earth.

Paul's mission was for us to understand the fullness of our Christ-life, our new identity AS Him. He had one concern: not that we would go too far in understanding the completeness of our co-identity, but that we wouldn't go far enough.

2 Corinthians 11:3 says, "I fear lest somehow as the serpent deceived Eve by his craftiness, so your minds (your perceptions) may be corrupted from the simplicity (the singleness, or oneness) that is in Christ." What is Paul talking about? He is concerned that we might lose the understanding of our singleness, our oneness, which is our identity IN Christ. This is the essence of the Gospel—the revelation of who we are now because of what Christ has done. Because of what He FINISHED for us and as us.

It's about who we've been resurrected AS... NOT who we've been resurrected to BECOME.

1 Corinthians 6:17 says, *"He who is joined to the Lord is one spirit with HIM."*

It doesn't say one spirit 'with' Him, as most translations suggest. The word 'with' was added by translators, likely because they struggled to grasp this single identity that we share with Christ. It says he who is joined to the Lord is one spirit. Paul's talking about a single identity. We are one spirit—Him. It's not two separate spirits... ours and His. It's one spirit... His. We're not with but IN. And because we are IN Him and He is IN us, we are fused together as ONE spirit. A shared single identity with Him. What a beautiful mystical truth.

Our new identity IN Christ is His identity IN us. One single identity —His life IN us and AS us.

If we're going to experience the fullness of our inheritance, such as restored health, wholeness, prosperity, etc., we must embrace this single identity as Him. And not just in our spirit only. Our soul is fully redeemed and has a single shared identity AS Him. We have the mind of Christ. The Amplified Bible says that we have the thoughts, feelings, and purposes of His heart or His mind. It doesn't say that we are to learn and emulate His thoughts, feelings, and purposes. It says we have the mind of Christ.

Our body is also fully redeemed. It is a single identity AS Him. We are the embodiment of Him—He lives IN us. Ephesians 5:30 says that we are members (limbs and parts) of His body. Then Paul emphasizes something incredible so that we won't miss the significance of it! He says we are OF HIS FLESH AND OF HIS BONES. Jesus, in Luke 24:39, spoke to the disciples, "Touch me for a spirit hath NOT flesh and bones." The Mirror Bible notes that the resurrection of Jesus did not compromise the incarnation. Resurrection life is packaged in skin and bones. Ezekiel said it like this, "there's a Man on the throne!"

Our flesh and bone body co-resurrected the same AS His... immortal, incorruptible, and ageless! Not apart from His... but resurrected AS ONE body... His. His life IN us is our identity... it defines our physical body.

Romans 7:4 says, *"Therefore, my brethren, you also have become dead to the law through the body of Christ that you may be married to another. To*

Him who was raised from the dead that you
should bear fruit to God."

The word 'married' is ginomai, which means to become, cause to be, or emerge. It signifies a change of condition, state of being, or place. We are married to Another. We became or emerged as Another. And who is the Another? HIM, who was raised from the dead.

We emerged or became Him who was raised from the dead. Because His life in us is our life. WOW!

John said it like this, "AS He is, so are we in this world." Not as He was in the gospels, but as He is resurrected from the dead. It was the physical body of Jesus that was raised from the dead. 1 Peter 3:18-19 tells us that Jesus was made alive in the spirit when He went and preached to the spirits in prison. BUT He was made alive physically when He was raised. And the declaration here in Romans 7:4 is that when we emerged from our co-death with Him, we resurrected AS Him who was raised from the dead. We are His flesh and His bones. The old man had died in all of its corruption.

The new man is alive with His life, AS HIM—a reflection of Him in the earth—incorruptible, immortal, sinless, the perfect image and likeness of Abba.

Let's take this a step further. Romans 6:9 says, "Knowing that Christ, having been raised from the dead, dies no more; death no longer has dominion over Him." WOW! Let's read this the way Holy Spirit intended us to read this. We often see these verses as describing the wonderful things that happened to Jesus because of His death and resurrection. But Jesus didn't need any of those things—we did! He had all of that before He emptied Himself and came to secure it to us. He died and resurrected for us and *as us* because we needed these glorious things.

This verse starts with, "Knowing that Christ having been raised from the dead." Who have we become according to Romans 7:4? We became Another, **Him who was raised from the dead**. We need to start inserting our name in these verses. So, knowing that Christ (which includes us because we share His identity) has been raised from the dead, dies no more, death no longer has dominion.

Death is not just physical death. It includes sickness, disease, accidents, poverty, affliction, fear, etc. Death no longer has dominion over Him. This isn't just excellent news about Him. This is excellent news about us! Death (in all of its manifestations) NO LONGER have dominion over us.

This isn't just excellent news about Him. This is excellent news about us!

So, what should be our expectation in life? What should be the expectations of our physical body? We were raised from the dead! We are free from death and ALL its manifestations—sickness, disease, poverty, addiction, etc. This is our identity. His identity is our identity. We are IN Him, and He is IN us... *a single co-identity!*

He is Christ. We are Christ. How? BECAUSE we are His and in complete union with Him—ONE!

1 Corinthians 12:27 says, "Now you are the body of Christ and members in particular." Make it personal, not just corporate... "Now, I am the body of Christ and a member individually. I am the physical body of Christ, His flesh, and His bones."

The Mirror Bible says it this way, "*You are the body of Christ, **individually as much as you are his body corporately**. Every one of you mirrors him. He defines your form.*" [emphasis mine]

In Galatians 6:17, Paul says, "From now on, let no one trouble me, for I bear in my body the marks of Jesus." Religion will tell you this refers to all the bruising and beatings Paul took in his persecution. But go deeper into this. Paul had a profound revelation of his co-identity with Christ. Everything he speaks comes from his understanding and revelation of his true identity "as Him who was raised from the dead" (Romans 7:4). He knew he bore the marks of the Lord Jesus in his body, not just because of physical beatings but because of his deep spiritual union with Christ.

Paul's statement—"From now on, let no one trouble me, for I bear the marks of the Lord Jesus in my body"—is not just about his persecutions. The Greek word for "no one" is médeis, which can be translated as either no one or nothing.

Make it personal. Don't just read it as Paul's experience. Insert yourself in these truths and see your own co-identity with Christ, AS Christ.

In other words, from now on, NOTHING gives me trouble, for I bear in my body the marks of Jesus. Cancer can't trouble me! Heart disease can't trouble me! Addiction and manic depression can't trouble me!

Why? Because I bear in my body the marks of Jesus. His marks are my co-marks. His suffering was my co-suffering.

Our identity in Him is a co-identity—a single shared identity.

We've become Him who was raised from the dead (Romans 7:4) and we bear in our body the marks of Jesus (Galatians 6:17). Therefore, any difference between your physical body and His physical body is indistinguishable. We are members of His body, of His flesh, and His bones. This is our co-identity. We have become, we emerged AS Him who was raised from the dead.

So, any difference between our bodies and His body is ONLY distinguishable in our perception. Because, in truth, we were raised in newness of life. So why is our perception distorted? Could it be that the two most unreliable, deceived, corrupt information systems (the world and religion) have determined our health and life expectancy for us? We have listened to their definitions of what our life should look like instead of understanding that His life is our life. And whatever is true of Him is equally true of us.

What is true of Him? He is immortal, incorruptible, and ageless. This is the truth of our co-identity in Christ—sharing in His victory, His life, and His eternal nature.

But the church started telling people that their life expectancy should be 70 or 80 years, basing it on Psalm 90. But Moses was about 120 when he prayed this in Psalm 90. He was lamenting over the fact people around him were dying around 70 or 80 years old. He was having to bury "kids" in the wilderness that were 50 years younger than him. Then, the church changed it and began to teach that God's will for man's lifespan is 120 years based on Genesis 6:3. But that wasn't the will of God, He wasn't setting a cap for our life expectancy. This verse is talking about the flood. And Noah lived 500 plus years AFTER the flood.

The world's understanding of our lifespan is no different. Their numbers are constantly changing based on natural conditions and circumstances. So, we've allowed the world and religion to define for us our health and life expectancy instead of understanding that *as He is, so are we in this world...* immortal, incorruptible, and ageless. The church and the world don't get to determine our quality of life.

No one and nothing gets to decide what our life span is. Why? Because death has no dominion over us.

Romans 12:1–2 says, "*I beseech you therefore, brethren, by the mercies of God, that ye present your bodies a living sacrifice, holy, acceptable unto God, which is your reasonable service ² And be not conformed to this world: but be ye transformed by the renewing of your mind, that ye may prove what is that good, and acceptable, and perfect, will of God.*"

Paul said, "present your bodies." This is the same Paul who told us in Galatians that we are members of His body, of His flesh, and of His bones. The same Paul who said in Romans that we have become Him who was raised from the dead. Now Paul says, present your bodies as a living sacrifice. Religion tells us we must do something sacrificial to actually become. But there is only one Living Sacrifice—Jesus. So, what's Paul saying here? He's saying to present yourself as Him. The word 'present' is paristémi, which means to stand beside, to show, and to substantiate.

In other words, he's saying stand beside your body and recognize it as the body of Christ, the Living Sacrifice who took our bodies into His own.

The same word 'present' is used in Colossians 1: "Him we preach that we may present every man perfect in Christ Jesus."

Paul is urging us to stand beside ourselves, to remember who we are. Stand beside ourselves and get a good view of our true identity— whatever defines His body now defines yours. His identity is your identity. You've become Another. You emerged from death, co-resurrected as Him who was raised from the dead.

This is not blasphemy. It's not heresy. It's way outside the box that religion and the world have placed us in, but it's the truth. This is who we are.

This is not blasphemy. It's not heresy. It's way outside the box that religion and the world have placed us in, but it's the truth. This is who we are.

Paul said, "It's no longer I who live but Christ." He also said, "For me to live is Christ." Paul's life was Christ. His identity was Christ. Was Paul exalting himself above Christ? Was he denying the supremacy of Jesus Christ? No, absolutely not. Paul simply understood that he was baptized in Christ. He was immersed in Christ.

The word 'baptize' is *baptizo*, meaning to immerse. But it also meant more than simply dunking an object in water or liquid. In the cloth industry, it meant to immerse cloth into a vat of dye, causing the cloth to take on the characteristics of the dye liquid. In other words, the cloth absorbed the color of the dye, becoming that same color. So, in the religious realm, when Jews walked into the Mikveh (the ritual cleansing bath), the understanding was that they took on the qualities of the Living Water they were immersed in, becoming pure and clean.

That's single co-identity—understanding we are AS HIM in this world.

Paul isn't just talking about us being one spirit AS Christ. He was speaking out of an understanding and a revelation that we are also of His flesh and His bones. Jesus gave Himself AS us so that we could be raised AS Him who was raised from the dead. Paul said when you stand beside yourself and recognize your body to be the body of Christ, the Living Sacrifice, understanding that His resurrection was your resurrection, THEN you will give substance to His claims. In other words, you will give substance to the tangible experience of this newness of life—your Christ life. Present yourself, stand beside yourself, and give substance to this co-identity. Look in the mirror and say, "Wow, that's the risen Christ looking back at me!"

Paul's not telling you to do something sacrificial to become. He's saying this is who you are NOW because of the mercies of the living God. We co-identify with Christ—sharing His identity. We are AS Christ. What is true of Him is equally true of us! We are baptized INTO Him.

This revelation is spreading by the grace of God into all the earth. The knowledge of our co-identity is growing in the hearts of those who are genuinely dissatisfied with the religious experience they've had. They are truly desiring and seeking the Lord's wisdom and revelation. They are beholding Him, and in beholding Him, they are seeing themselves as they really are.

2 Corinthians 4:3 says, *"But if our gospel be hid, it is hid to them that are perishing."* The good news of our Christ-life is hidden to those who are perishing.

Paul's not talking in an "us and them" language in the sense of "church and world." In other words, those perishing are not who religion has deemed as those perishing... i.e., the prostitute, the drug addict, the person who blasphemes God, the Muslim, etc. That's a religious "us and them" mentality. That's a language that God doesn't speak.

The word 'perishing' is apollumi and means to lose, destroy, or die. It is to wander and live a life of non-existence, not participating in the life God had designed for us. Jesus said in Luke 19:10 that He came to seek and save that which was perishing. What did Jesus come to seek and save? Our lost identity. The Mirror Bible says it like this, "I have come to their rescue and will help them rediscover their authentic identity and redeemed innocence!" Perishing is walking in the distorted, false identity.

Paul goes on in verse 4 to say that the god of this world (i.e., the religious systems of this world) has blinded people's minds in unbelief. Why? For fear that the light of the glorious gospel of Christ, who is the image of God, would shine on them. In other words, the world's religious systems blinded people's minds in unbelief so that they would not recognize and experience the life of Christ *in* them. The Mirror Bible says, "The veil of unbelief obstructs a person's view and keeps them from seeing what the light of the gospel so clearly reveals: the glory of God in the image and likeness of our Maker redeemed in human form; this is what the gospel of Christ is all about."

Did Paul say that it was sickness, disease, old age, cancer, Alzheimer's, etc., causing men to perish? No, he said it was ONE THING and one thing only—blinded perception. In other words, religion has blinded minds with unbelief regarding their co-identity with Christ. He said their perception has been blinded lest the revelation of the good news, glory, presence, and power of Christ, the image of God should dawn on them. Is he just talking about us getting a revelation of the fact that Christ is the image of God? No, unbelieving religious systems will even tell you Christ is the image of God. That doesn't require any tremendous heavy-duty revelation.

The emphasis here is on this truth dawning on you—that you realize that you are the glorious image of God *in Christ*.

And then he goes on in verse 6, and the Mirror Bible says it so well. It says, "The light source is founded in the same God who said, 'Light, be!'

And light shone out of darkness! He lit the lamp in our understanding so that we may clearly recognize the features of his likeness in the face of Jesus Christ reflected within us." And then IMMEDIATELY after that, he says in verse 7, "We have this treasure in earthen vessels." What is the treasure? The identity of Christ, the glory of God. And glory is the view and opinion and manifested presence of God. And where is this treasure, this image, and likeness of Christ? In our physical bodies!

And in verse 10, Paul says, "Always bearing about the dying of the Lord Jesus in the body." Why? He says so that the life also of Jesus might be made manifest in our body. Not in heaven someday. No, he said the LIFE of Jesus, the One who lives and dies no more, the One who defeated death and is incorruptible and immortal is made manifest in our physical bodies! St. Athanasius said, *"through death deathlessness has been made known to us."*

Glory to God! This is good news… the almost too good to be true news that makes a man jump for joy!

So, just how blinded has our perception been? Knowing all this, what should be the life and health expectation of Him who was raised from the dead? In other words, what would you say the health and life expectancy of Jesus should be? Well, He lives forever, never defeated, never sick, always victorious, everything He says comes to pass, etc. And the beautiful truth of our co-identity with Christ is that WE have been caused to be Him who was raised from the dead.

What should our life and health expectancy be? I think it should start with these words, "death no longer has dominion over me." And then write down EVERYTHING that qualifies as death, destruction, losing, perishing, sickness, disease, financial ruin or loss, addiction, fear, etc., knowing that those things have no dominion over you. IT IS FINISHED!

This becomes your new expectation—a life fully grounded in the reality that IT IS FINISHED!

Chapter 19

The Power of Hope!

Expectations shape our reality. When it comes to healing or embracing God's promises, we've often made it all about our faith—questioning if it's strong enough or if we possess enough of it. Yet, we overlook a crucial truth: His faith secured everything for us. His faith FINISHED it all for us and as us. Every blessing and promise we seek to manifest in our lives is already within us. As Hebrews 11:1 declares, "Now faith is the substance of things hoped for, the evidence of things not seen."

I love how the Mirror translation puts it: "*Persuasion confirms confident expectation and proves the unseen world to be more real than the seen. Faith celebrates as certain what hope visualizes as future.*"

Hope is our expectation, and in Greek, the word for hope is *elpis*, meaning confident expectation. It signifies the anticipation of what is sure or certain—the reality of what Christ FINISHED. Hope is the eager anticipation and expectation of the tangible manifestation of His completed work in our lives.

What is the difference between faith and hope?

Faith, from the Greek *pistis*, means persuasion, conviction, or belief. Hope is to anticipate and expect that which we're persuaded of. Do you see the difference? We can be persuaded of something but not necessarily be expecting it in our lives. Many people are persuaded that God heals and believe the verse that says, "By His stripes, we are healed." So, it's possible to believe, be deeply convinced about something, be fully persuaded, and YET not obtain the tangible results of the FINISHED work of Jesus Christ. Why? Because we don't have the expectation and anticipation of that becoming a part of our life here and now.

Hope is not wishful thinking. It is a confident expectation grounded in the reality of Christ's finished work. It's more than just believing in the promises; it's about eagerly anticipating their manifestation in our lives. Faith provides the substance, the foundation of what we hope for, but hope itself is the joyful, expectant attitude that brings those promises into our tangible reality.

When we truly grasp this, it transforms our approach to life. We no longer pray out of desperation or doubt but out of a deep, unwavering assurance that what we hope for is already ours in Christ. This shift in perspective is powerful. It moves us from striving to resting, from doubting to celebrating, and from longing to receiving.

I couldn't write a book on New Covenant healing without dedicating a chapter to hope, the power that accesses the unseen realm. This subject alone could fill an entire book. Covering every aspect of hope in one chapter is impossible. So, I won't delve into all the verses mentioning hope or explore the role of patience with hope. Maybe one day, I'll write a book solely on hope. For now, let's focus on how hope expresses itself through our lives, particularly through our great boldness of speech, as highlighted in 2 Corinthians.

Hebrews 6:11 says, "*And we desire that each one of you show the same diligence to the full assurance of hope until the end.*"

The word 'assurance' in Greek is *plérophoreó*, meaning the full carry through. Its root signifies the accomplishment or completion of something. The word 'end' is *telos*, meaning to reach the end goal or purpose. In other words, we desire the fullness of hope to the end.

We are to be diligent—zealous, eager, or quick—in the full accomplishment and completion of our expectation until the goal is attained. We are called to rest, but even in our rest, we participate in the accomplishment of our expectation, as described in Hebrews 6. This isn't about works; it's about living a life of co-participation, expecting the manifestation of the FINISHED works of Christ in our lives.

Hope is not passive; it's active and powerful. It fuels our bold declarations and confident expectations, aligning our lives with the completed work of Christ. As we embrace hope, we co-participate with Him, seeing His promises manifest in our lives. This is the power of hope—a driving force that brings the unseen into the seen, the eternal into the now, and the promise into reality.

Each of us is being exhorted to show diligence in accomplishing or reaching the end of our hope. What is the end of our hope? The tangible manifestation of His FINISHED works in our life. Our hope should not be that Jesus will heal us because Jesus already healed us two thousand years ago. He's already FINISHED ALL things. We can confidently expect the tangible, manifested results of His FINISHED work in our lives. We can confidently expect divine health that is *in* us to be our experience in life.

So, how do we show diligence in accomplishing that hope? How do we bring what is FINISHED into reality in our lives?

2 Corinthians 3:12 says, "*Therefore, since we have such hope, we use great boldness of speech.*"

Since we have this intense anticipation and expectation of the tangible, manifested FINISHED work in our lives, we use speech to produce that experience. Hope isn't just a confident expectation in our thoughts or imagination. That is important, but our hope, our confident expectation, is expressed through our words. Jesus said in Luke that it is with our mouth, with our speech, that we bring forth the treasure in our hearts.

The Greek word for "bring forth" is *prophero*, which means to bring the goal forward. It is to bring the treasure we have in us (the FINISHED works that He did) into necessary tangible manifestation. Our words are powerful. The Hebrew sages say that in Genesis, Adam being made a living being was Adam being made as a speaking spirit just like God. Hebrews 11:3 says that the worlds were framed by the spoken word (*rhema*) of God so that which is seen was made from that which is unseen. The power of hope accesses the unseen realm. Hebrews 6:9 says that hope enters the Presence behind the veil, going into the most holy place where ALL is FINISHED in us.

Our speech brings forth what is unseen into tangible manifestation, producing the experience of IT IS FINISHED in our lives.

Hebrews 10:23 says, *"Let us hold fast the confession of our faith without wavering for He who promised is faithful."*

The word 'confession' can trigger many, but remember, this isn't about works or formulas to "get healed." We're talking about co-participating with God from a position of rest regarding His FINISHED work in us. We are co-seated with Him, living a life of union with Him—a life of co. There is a designed mechanism given to us to provide tangibility and manifestation of the hope we possess within us. Our speech, our confession, can't be works because Hebrews 4 tells us that God rested, His works were FINISHED before the foundation of the world. In rest, He framed the worlds or spoke them into existence. Similarly, our speech, our confession, is from our co-seated position in rest.

Hebrews 10:23 in our Bibles says that we are to hold fast the confession of our faith. But in Greek, it says, "hold fast the confession of our hope." We are to hold fast the confession of our hope without wavering because He who promised is faithful. The word 'confession' is *homologeo*, meaning agreement. Our confession springs from our HOPE, not just a list of promises. Our hope is Christ, and our confession is agreeing with His FINISHED work. The writer of Hebrews said, "Let us hold fast the confession of our hope." In other words, let us speak the same thing as our hope.

Since Christ is our hope, and He said it is FINISHED, our confession is the confident expectation of the tangible manifestation of what He FINISHED. One of the tangible manifestations of what He FINISHED that we want to experience in our life is our divine health, our wholeness. Our bodies are pre-wired to respond to our voices. They have receptors that respond to what we say. Our bodies have an obligation to respond—positively and negatively. We are always speaking; we are always confessing. Instead of a confession of hope, we often hold fast to a confession of natural circumstances. Our bodies respond to what we speak.

It's so important that we grasp this!

We haven't realized that the life we're living now has been created with our expectations, with our speech or our confession. We think our lives just somehow happened, that we were born into this, and it would have been no matter what we had done. We haven't realized that we've created the experiences we're having right now with the words of our mouths and the agreement of our hearts. We are the gatekeepers of our lives. What we allow into our hearts and choose to think about will work itself out into our experience because what we think about will eventually come out of our mouths. Instead of agreeing with God and His FINISHED work manifesting in our lives, we often agree with the systems of this world and their natural conclusions, speaking those as conclusions, and then those conclusions (aging, sickness, disease, death, lack, etc.) become our expectations and manifest in our lives.

Living a life of co-participation with God means resting in a different expectation for our lives—an expectation of the tangible manifestation of what He FINISHED for us and in us: immortality, divine health, wholeness, prosperity, etc. It requires diligence, not by works, but through continual engagement with Holy Spirit as He leads us to make the change and turn. James said the tongue is like a rudder on a ship, and we need to use our tongue, our bold confession of hope, to change the course of our life.

Hebrews 4:16 says, "Let us, therefore, come with all boldness to the throne of grace that we may obtain mercy and find grace to help in time of need." The word 'boldness' is *parrésia*, meaning confidence or freedom of speech. It is to speak bluntly, assuredly, and with fearless resolve. We are to come to the throne of grace with all confidence and freedom, speaking bluntly and with fearless resolve, announcing God's grace. We come declaring that the grace of God, what Christ has FINISHED for us and as us, will manifest in our life. Our circumstances make no difference. He said we will obtain it or receive it (*lambano* in Greek). We will immediately lay hold of what is already ours because He already laid hold of it for us, *as us!* FINISHED!

The Mirror Bible says, "*For this reason, we can approach the authoritative throne of grace with bold utterance. We are welcome there in His embrace and are reinforced with imme-diate effect in times of trouble.*"

Hebrews 10:19 says, "*Therefore brethren having boldness to enter the holiest by the blood of Jesus.*"

Remember, this word boldness always refers to our speech in its definition. It says we have bold speech to enter the holiest by the blood of Jesus.

The Mirror Bible says, "*So, fellow family, what the blood of Jesus communicates, seals our immediate access into this ultimate place of sacred encounter with unashamed confidence.*"

Our boldness of speech is declaring what Jesus communicates—it is FINISHED! Hebrews 6:19 talks about how hope enters the Presence behind the veil where the forerunner, Jesus, has gone and entered for us. The Presence behind the veil refers to the most holy place. It's the most sanctified, the most set-apart place. It's the place of God's Presence. It's entirely separated from the world—from the corruption of sin and death. The holiest place, the place behind the veil, the place of God's presence, is *in* us. It's where ALL things that pertain to life and godliness, every spiritual blessing, ALL His FINISHED works are contained... in us!

We have been given boldness—bold speech—to enter the holy place. Hebrews 6:19 says that hope enters this holy place. Our declaration of hope, confident expectation of experiencing the FINISHED work in our lives, enters this place where ALL things pertaining to life and godliness are contained. In truth, there is no veil separating this most holy place. Jesus, in His declaration of "It is FINISHED," rent the veil! Hebrews 10:20 says we enter this veil "by His new and living way through the veil that is His flesh."

The only way to enter through the veil is through His flesh. Carnal thinking and speaking cannot access the most holy place where His

FINISHED works are. Hebrews 6 tells us that our hope (our confident expectation of the tangible, manifested FINISHED works in our life) accesses the Presence behind the veil. Hebrews 10 adds that our bold speech—our declaration of hope, our confident expectation of these tangible, manifested works—accesses this most holy place, the unseen realm within us.

The writer of Hebrews reveals that we have been given something specially designed to enter behind the veil. This gift carries us beyond the opposition of the flesh and the natural realm into the holiest place where FINISHED dwells IN us, bringing forth FINISHED into our life experiences. To make the tangible manifestation of FINISHED our reality, we use our confession of hope.

Our confession is designed to bring everything Christ has placed IN us into natural physical manifestation. You may not always feel bold, but He has given you boldness of speech—a firm resolve of IT IS FINISHED in your life! He has equipped you with bold speech to bring His FINISHED work into natural manifestation. He didn't give you a list of dos and don'ts to enter the most holy place.

Isaiah 26:12 says that He FINISHED all our works for us. There is nothing left for us to do. But He equipped us with our bold confession of hope so that we can co-participate with Him in living a FINISHED life! Our bold confession of hope is a powerful gift from Him in us. Confession has been abused and consequently criticized over the years as just a positive mind over matter or a "name it and claim it" message. But this is what we've been given—we have boldness of speech to enter the most holiest place by the blood of Jesus, or by His communication of IT IS FINISHED! We don't enter the holiest place by our works, our formulas, etc. We enter by what He has given us – our bold confession of "It is FINISHED in my life, in my tangible experiences." Which really is His FINISHED confession in us! That's all it takes. It really is such a simple thing. We have this confession because He created it for us, and it was created by His accomplishments.

Hebrews 3:1 says, "*Therefore, holy brethren partakers of the heavenly calling consider the Apostle and High Priest of our confession Christ Jesus.*"

The Mirror Bible says, "*...acquaint yourselves immediately and fully with Christ Jesus as the Ambassador and Chief Priest of our confession. Our lives co-echo the logic of God's eternal conversation in Him.*"

I love that... co-echo. Our lives are a life of co with Abba. Our confession is co-echoing His eternal conversation in Jesus. What is His eternal conversation? It is FINISHED, and He is SEATED! Jesus is the One that created our confession for us. He is the SEATED High Priest of our confession. That tells us that our confession of hope, the expectation of His FINISHED results in our lives, is always connected to rest, not works. Our confession is totally built upon His accomplishments, and it's His integrity that sustains it. It's His FINISHED confession IN us.

In Deuteronomy chapter 30:11–14, Moses said, "*For

this commandment which I command you today
is not too mysterious for you, nor is it far off. ^{12} It is
not in heaven that you should say, 'Who will
ascend into heaven for us and bring it to us, that
we may hear it and do it?' ^{13} Nor is it beyond the
sea that you should say, 'Who will go over the sea
for us and bring it to us, that we may hear it and
do it?' ^{14} But the word is very near you, in your
mouth and in your heart, that you may do it."

He said the word is not too mysterious for you. Some translations say it's not hidden from you or not too difficult for you. What he's telling us is that the word in us is not a difficult thing. It's not mysterious, it's not hidden from us, it's not some mystical thing. It's not far off. It's in our heart and in our mouths. He said it's not in heaven that we should say who will ascend into heaven for us and bring it to us so that we may hear it and do it. And then he goes on, saying that it's not beyond the sea that we should say, "and who will go over the sea for us and bring it to us so that we may hear it and do it?"

We're clearly being told way back here in Deuteronomy that the fulfillment or production of the fruit of the word in our life comes from the Word that is in our mouth and in our hearts—it is the bold confession of our hope—FINISHED!

This is where our hope is fully accomplished—it's in your mouth and in your heart. **YOUR mouth and YOUR heart**. It's not the word of your pastor, your favorite televangelist, or even your favorite author! And yet, people are still running from meeting to meeting, from person to person, trying to get healed. They'll be prayed for by one minister, and then they make plans to go and be prayed for by another minister right away. What are they doing? They're going over the sea and up into the heavens like Moses said. When all along, the word is with them in their heart and in their mouth. And it's lying dormant in them.

I'm not saying you don't ask for people to pray for you. But we've got to start trusting that the word that will bring forth the tangible manifested experience of healing, prosperity, or peace in our lives is IN us... It's in our hearts, and it's in our mouths already. It's a bold confession of hope that God has given to us.confession of hope that God has given to us.

Paul in Romans 10:6 says, "But the righteousness of faith speaks in this way, do not say in your heart who will ascend into heaven that is to bring Christ down from above." Paul is rephrasing that Deuteronomy passage and bringing us to the FINISHED work of Christ. He's telling us how we are to speak. When we understand that our righteousness is by the faith of Jesus Christ and not by our own works, then we won't say in our hearts who will ascend into heaven to bring Christ down.

In other words, when we understand that it's about Christ's FINISHED works and His faith, we won't ask Christ "to come" and heal us. We won't be looking for others to pray for us or "ascend into the heavens" for us. We won't be looking for someone righteous enough to be able to get in touch with God or make contact with God on our behalf. We won't be looking for someone who has a great anointing so that we can get healed.

You know who's anointed enough? YOU are! And I am! We ALL are!

Because it's His anointing IN us. It's His anointing that FINISHED everything for you and as you. He's also saying, "Stop saying what ritual do I need to do or observe to get Christ to come down from above and heal me? Do I need to fast, or do I need to go into intercessory prayer for a long period of time?" And stop saying, "What do I need to do or who do I need to go see to get Jesus to come down and heal me?" We don't need to find someone more righteous or anointed to pray for us because all you need to access your divine health and wholeness is IN you. ALL that is necessary to accomplish everything outwardly that Jesus accomplished inwardly is in your mouth and in your heart! It's not in 17 more tape sets or 15 more healing crusades. And it's not even in one more of my books! Each and every one of us is capable of bringing the FINISHED work of Jesus Christ into experiential reality in our life simply by trusting His word of FINISHED in our hearts and beginning to speak it with our mouths.

I love these verses in the Mirror Bible. Verses 6–7: "Faith announces that the Messiah is no longer a distant promise; neither is he reduced to a mere historical hero. He is mankind's righteousness now! The revelation of what God accomplished in Christ births a new conversation! The old type of guess-talk has become totally irrelevant; Christ is not hiding somewhere in the realm of heaven as a future hope; so, to continue to say, 'Who will ascend into heaven, to bring Christ down,' makes no sense at all! (The nearness of the Word in incarnation language is the new conversation! The word made flesh so that all flesh may witness the glory of God reflected in the radiance of their own illuminated understanding!) [7] Faith-conversation understands the resurrection-revelation (and mankind's co-inclusion in it! Hosea 6:2)."

And the last part of verse 8 in the Mirror Bible says, "The Word is extremely close to you. It spills over from your heart and becomes dynamic conversation in your mouth!"

He has given us His bold FINISHED confession.

Our bold declaration of hope, of the confident expectation and anticipation of the tangible manifestation of living a FINISHED life, is His FINISHED confession in our heart and in our mouth. A life experience of the abundant life that we've been given IN Christ. A life that is His life... immortal, incorruptible, whole, restored to health, prosperous, etc. This confession is in our hearts and overflows out of our mouths!

And verse 9 in the Mirror Bible says, *"Now your salvation is realized! Your own words echo God's voice. The unveiling of the masterful act of Jesus forms the words in your mouth, inspired by the conviction in your heart that God indeed raised him from the dead."*

Our co-echo of the expectation of FINISHED in our lives enters the veil of the Presence. It enters the holiest place of FINISHED. And our salvation is realized; it manifests in our life! Our divine health is realized! Our wholeness is realized! Our prosperity is realized!

All that is in us begins to manifest when we are simply giving glory to God by resting in Him and boldly declaring that we confidently anticipate and welcome the tangible manifestation of what He FINISHED in our lives.

Chapter 20

Praise Silences the Enemy

Psalm 8 is one of my favorite Psalms. God created man a little lower than Himself. If your Bible says a little lower than angels, cross out angels and put God. In Hebrew, the word isn't angels; it is *Elohim* (the Triune God: Father, Son, and Holy Spirit). We've been created by God a little lower than Himself and crowned with glory and honor! But if we don't understand that we are the image and likeness of God, crowned with glory and honor, and given dominion over the works of His hands and that ALL things are under our feet, we will walk through life in a fallen, distorted sense of identity as Adam did. We won't understand that we are ordained to co-participate with God in co-creating or framing our worlds.

Instead, we'll accept an inferior role of a servant rather than a son, feeling powerless to the world around us and the circumstances that come our way. And that's what's happened to so many of the body of Christ. They have just settled into role-playing as servants of God. Waiting on Him to change their circumstances, crying out to Him to deliver them, or warring against things that He already FINISHED for us and as us... sin, sickness, death, disease, poverty, etc. He created us as lords of our earth. Lords of our health, finances, peace, etc. Lord of our life, of our sphere of influence. Or as Paul says in Galatians, which is one of my favorite terms, "masters of ALL!"

We are not servants. We are not slaves enslaved to anything. And we are not powerless in life! We are lords, kings, sons, co-heirs, masters of ALL!

This Psalm is all about us! It's our birth certificate, so to speak. It gives us a broader glimpse of being made in His image and likeness. This is Abba, through David, boasting about His kids. The writer of Hebrews quotes Psalm 8:4–6.

The Mirror Bible translation of Hebrews 2:6–8 is so good. It says, *"What is it about the human species that God cannot get them out of his mind? What does He see in the son of man that so captivates his gaze? [7] It seems that man briefly descends to a less elevated place than Elohim; yet he is crowned with God's own glory and dignity and appointed in a position of authority over all the works of his hands. [8] God's intention was that human life should rule the planet. He subjected everything without exception to his control."*

Isn't that beautiful?! This is how Abba feels about us! He has always been so captivated with us that He can't get us out of His mind! He's enthralled with us! We are His crowning glory of creation! We are His pièce de résistance! And He placed us in a position of lordship over ALL the works of His hands. And just in case we were to miss the immensity of that, the writer of Hebrews repeats it by saying that He subjected EVERYTHING WITHOUT EXCEPTION under our feet!

Verses one and nine in this Psalm are beautiful matching bookends. They begin and wrap all of this up for us in the "excellency or the majesty of His name in all the earth." I love the deeper message in that. We start in the excellency, in the majesty of His name (His Divine Nature). Ephesians 1:4 says, "We were chosen IN Christ before the foundation of the world." And no matter how far men fell in their understanding, no matter how far we roam from our identity of His nature IN us, it still continues to define us in the end. Yes, this is saying, God is excellent. That's a given. But is earth talking just about our physical planet earth? Or is it talking about us! Remember in Genesis, we were told that we were made of the dust of the earth.

> So, *in* all our earth, *in* all our physical being, His
> Name is excellent! It's majestic!

And then, from that understanding of His Name IN us, we can see that this is also saying to us how excellent our name is in all the physical earth! He has made our name great! He has made our name excellent! Isn't that what He told Abraham in Genesis 12? So, His excellent Name IN us has made us majestic and excellent in relationship to all the earth. Not just the physical world we live in, but in connection to everything in our sphere of influence... our health, finances, relationships, etc.

His Name IN us has given us the majesty of dominion. His Name IN us has given us a new identity. We are an excellent, majestic creation! We are not powerless in our dominion, in our world.

Begin to speak to your earth that not only are you excellent, but you are majestic. Speak to your finances, health, and emotions, and begin to say that you have been made a lord by the Lord of lords. And you have been made a king by the King of kings. The Moffatt Translation says, "he (mankind) is crowned king of nature, invested with a divine authority over creation." By virtue of His Name IN you, we are masters of all circumstances and situations. This is our identity! Psalm 8 tells us that we've been given His name, His likeness, and His estate. And we have been made lords over ALL of His creation. What more could we possibly need or want?

I love the Mirror Bible's translation of the phrase "made a little lower than God." It says: "It seems that man briefly descends to a less elevated place than Elohim, yet he is crowned with God's own glory and dignity and appointed in a position of authority over all the works of his hands."

The writer of Hebrews, when quoting Psalm 8, said something similar, he said, "When God subjected all things to him, He left nothing outside of his control." Yet, at present, we do not see everything subject to him. We can see that something changed about mankind. He was crowned with glory and honor and given dominion over ALL the works of God's hands, but for a while, he briefly descended to a less elevated place than Elohim. This sounds like the fall. Mankind fell in their understanding of their identity as sons made in the image and likeness of God and as lords in the earth. Yet, they were still crowned with God's own glory and honor and had dominion over ALL things.

Nothing about humanity had changed except their own perception of themselves, God, and the world around them.

Psalm 8:2 says, "Out of the mouth of babes and nursing infants You have ordained strength, because of Your enemies, that You may silence the enemy and the avenger." This is really a key verse for us to understand how to live a victorious life. It reveals an enemy whose purpose is to rob us of the understanding of God's identity IN us and our dominion as lords in the earth. But it also tells us how to step out victoriously in these things... He has ordained strength in our mouth to silence the enemy and the avenger.

An enemy robbed humanity of the revelation of their identity. Depriving them of enjoying the greatness of their being, the excellence of their identity, and the experience of their lordship in all the earth. In Genesis 1:28, we're told there was a subduing of the earth prior to having dominion. And David says the same thing here in Psalm 8. In verse 2, subduing our earth is really what he is talking about. And then, in verse six, he begins to introduce dominion. The word 'subdue' is a word that means to trample underfoot, to conquer, to do injury to, and to bring into captivity.

So, just to be clear before we go on, I am not talking about spiritual warfare! We subdue our earth by subduing our carnal, sense realm thoughts. Paul told us in 2 Corinthians 10 to take every thought captive. Thoughts that exalt themselves above the knowledge of God.

The word 'thoughts' is the Greek word *noema*, meaning perceptions. And it's perceptual manipulation that the enemy uses to keep us from entering into the tangible manifestation of the FINISHED work in our lives. It's what he used in the garden of Eden with Eve. Implying that she was not complete. That she was lacking something of God in her identity.

Our perceptions determines our experiences in life.

Verse two says the enemy and the avenger. The word 'enemy' in Hebrew is *ayab* and means to be hostile or to be an adversary. Colossians 1:21 says that mankind was hostile in their minds. And the word 'avenger' is *naqam* and means vengeance, punishment, and revenge. The words enemy and avenger are both verbs in this verse. They are not nouns... they are not demonic entities or personalities.

So, again, please don't read into this that there is spiritual warfare that we need to engage in.

We have become so devil-conscious that we've missed understanding the real enemy: our distorted perception of God.

One day, I was reading Isaiah 53, and I saw that before it says, "By His stripes we were healed," it says, "We esteemed Him stricken, smitten by God, and afflicted." And Abba said to me, "It's a false, distorted perception of Me that hinders an experience of healing." Isaiah said we esteem Him. Mankind began seeing God as a Judge who required punishment for our wrong actions. And we esteemed the death of Jesus as God striking Him, smiting Him, afflicting Him, pouring out His wrath upon Him BECAUSE OF us. We thought Jesus took our punishment, SO THAT God wouldn't punish us! And that false, distorted perception of God is the enemy and avenger that robs us of our identity. It robs us of being able to see how beloved we are as sons! We can't see that Abba's gaze is captivated by us because His love for us is so great... and has always been so great!

He was never a Judge who was set on punishing us. He is the One who has always pursued mankind in love. He is the Lover who left the garden with Adam because He couldn't be without us!

If we perceive Him as vengeful, angry, and punishing, it's hard to see Him as majestic and excellent in all the earth, especially in our own lives. When something like sickness or disease comes against us, we struggle to be victorious because thoughts of punishment run through our minds, telling us that maybe we did something to cause this cancer or financial loss. Or maybe God is punishing us. This mindset prevents us from seeing that His Name IN us has made us majestic in all areas of our lives—our health, finances, relationships, etc. It hinders our ability to experience healing because we're unsure if He will heal us, or if we are even worthy of it.

Jesus said that no one knew the Father but the Son. And He came to earth to show us not only what our identity looks like as sons but also Abba's true identity as a good Father. He didn't leave anything out. He didn't show us a God of wrath, judgment, and punishment because that isn't who Abba is! The writer of Hebrews in chapter 1 tells us that Jesus was the FULL, COMPLETE expression of God. In other words, when you see Jesus, you see the Father. And then in Hebrews 2:8 we're told that when God subjected all things to mankind, He left nothing outside of his control. Yet at present, we do not see everything subject to him, he also adds in verse 9, but we see Jesus!

The Mirror Bible says, "Let us consider Him in such a way that we may clearly perceive what God is saying to mankind in Him."

What is God saying to mankind in Jesus? It is FINISHED! Everything that would hinder mankind from walking as lords in the earth, as beloved sons in His image and likeness, was nailed to the cross and died! If we're still seeing sin, sickness, disease, death, etc., it's because it's coming from our own perceptions. From God's (Father, Son, and Spirit) perspective, the fall and all that came with it no longer exist!

If we're going to walk in our identity and rule the works of God's hands we're going to have to silence the voice of the enemy.

What is the voice of the enemy? God is vengeful, angry, and He punishes those who disobey Him. How do we silence the enemy? With our own voice. Because out of our mouths, He has ordained strength, security, and majesty. And the good news is that He said He's ordained it in the mouths of babies and nursing infants! We don't have to be Bible scholars to walk in victory. It's His word IN our mouths. ALL we need to know is IT IS FINISHED. That word is the strength in our mouths to silence the voice of the enemy.

You don't need another Robin Smit book, or another teaching tape, or 50 more lessons of anything. You merely need to realize that YOUR mouth has been ordained and anointed by God to administer your security, your majesty, and your strength. God put everything you need IN your mouth. Because He said, you were created in His image and likeness.

Like God, you create with the words of your mouth because God creates with the words of His mouth.

Jesus rephrases Psalm 8:2 in Matthew 21, saying, "Out of the mouth of babes and infants, you have perfected praise." He didn't say "ordained strength." This rephrasing tells me that Jesus wants us to understand that majesty, security, and strength are administered through praise. In other words, praise is the perfect way to silence the voice of the enemy, to silence those thoughts that tell you God is not who He says He is, and therefore you are not who He says you are.

The word "perfected" in this verse means to complete thoroughly, including repair and adjustment, and to restore to good working order. The root of the word means in the here and now—presently! Immediately! That's the word Jesus uses. We are lords of our earth. We are not powerless. We have dominion over any circumstance or any storm that may arise. And praise in our mouth restores our situations and circumstances to good working order immediately!

I have learned that when physical or financial challenges come against me, I praise Him. I remember Whose I am and who I am. I lift my hands and thank Abba that He hasn't created my body for sickness and disease. He created it for divine health and wholeness. I believe that His word in MY MOUTH is effective in my life. I thank Him that He crowned me with glory and honor and that I walk in the power, excellency, and majesty of His Name IN me. And you know, it has never failed! It isn't long before my body starts displaying health again, and my finances turn around. I don't rush to the doctor (though I'm not against you doing whatever you need to do—there is no condemnation or judgment!). I'm talking about my experiences. I have found that out of my mouth, He has ordained and perfected praise to make the immediate necessary repairs and adjustments in my life.

Notice in Psalm 8:2 that it says that God may silence the enemy and the avenger. Hasn't He already done that?

Yes. Hebrews 2:14 says that He destroyed him who had the power of death that is the devil. And 1 John 3:8 says for this purpose, the Son of God was manifest that he might destroy the works of the devil. And we know that He FINISHED all, and God is at rest.

God in your mouth silences the enemy. In other words, it's the goodness and the faithfulness of God in your mouth, the FINISHED words of God that silence the lying, accusing thoughts that God is vengeful, punishing, and pours out wrath. It is the declaration of His faithfulness, goodness, and love—the declaration of IT IS FINISHED that silences the enemy.

We thought that as we are faithful to praise Him God will rebuke the devil and silence the enemy on my behalf. No. The enemy is already defeated, **and all the administration of your victory is in your mouth.** Praise means to tell a story. And out of our mouths, He has perfected the telling of a story. What is the story? It is FINISHED!

Matthew 21:9 says that the multitudes went before and those who followed cried out, saying Hosanna to the Son of David blessed is He who comes in the name of the Lord Hosanna in the highest. Verses 10 and 11 say that they were declaring "this is Jesus." They were confessing who He was.

Verse 12 says that Jesus went into the temple and drove out those who bought and sold there. He overturned the tables of the money-changers and the seats of those who sold doves. What was Jesus doing? He was overturning man's distorted idea of sacrifice and offerings being God's will.

He was challenging their false understanding of God as a vengeful, punishing Deity who demanded a sacrifice.

It was the praise of the multitudes in verses 9–11 that actually drew Jesus into the temple. Their praise preceded His entrance. Once He was in the temple, He began to drive out the defilements that were robbing people of life. Then, in verse 14, it says that the blind and the lame came to Him, and He healed them.

When the temple was cleansed of all that was robbing the people of life, healing and restoration took place.

This isn't about Him cleaning the temple by removing every little thing you ever do wrong. Instead, He drove out those things that were robbing His people of abundant life and enjoying the Presence of God in their lives. Praise opened the door for disease, sickness, addiction, poverty, etc., to be driven out of our lives.

Our body is the temple of the Holy Spirit. Praise in our mouths—telling His story—draws His FINISHED works into manifestation in our temples, driving out everything that robs us of abundant life.

Psalm 100 says that we enter His courts with praise. The word **court** is *chatsar* and is the blowing of a trumpet. The trumpet in Hebrew is the Awakening Blast. His praise IN our mouths awakens us to who He is IN us and as us. It awakens us to ALL that He FINISHED.

People ask me all the time how can I experience the tangible manifestations of a FINISHED life? It's simple! Praise! This is my passion! It's His word in my mouth. It's declaring His story—IT IS FINISHED! And it's not just His story, it's ours. We are forever included in His story. It's the beautiful life of "co" that we live IN God. His death, His resurrection, His life, His victory is all ours as well as His.

Paul said in 1 Corinthians 11:30 that many are sick, weak, and dying early in life, giving only one reason: "for THIS reason..." The reason is in verse 29: "not discerning the Lord's body." Our body is the Lord's body. Verse 28 says that we are to examine ourselves—not our behavior, as we've often been taught before taking communion. No! In chapter 13 of 1 Corinthians, verse 5, Paul says we are to examine ourselves to see that Christ is in us.

Many are weak, sick, and dying needlessly because they haven't understood that He took our body into His body in the resurrection. His death and resurrection are our death and resurrection. This is our story! This is praise!

So, how do we live the tangible, manifested experience of being healed, whole, and lacking nothing? It's through the bold confession of hope in our mouths. It is the bold declaration of our story—mine and His! Our co-story! Boldly proclaiming that I anticipate and expect to tangibly experience ALL of what He FINISHED for me and *as me!*

This is the powerful, transformative truth of our identity in Christ. Embrace it, declare it, and live it! Our lives are a testament to His finished work, and we are called to live in the fullness of His victory It is finished, and we are complete in Him!

Epilogue: The Power of Our Rest and Victory

In that day, when the Lord Yahweh has given you rest from your pain, trouble, and cruel bondage, you will jeer at the king of Babylon and recite this proverb: "Your oppressor has been stilled and your onslaught is over! The Lord Yahweh has shattered the staff of the wicked, the brutal rod of the rulers. With their unceasing blows they used it cruelly to strike down nations. They subdued nations in anger with unrelenting persecution. But now the whole earth rests and is at peace. It bursts out with singing."

— Isaiah 14:3-7 (Passion Translation)

Isaiah prophesied about that day, and I'm here to declare: we are living in that day! Two thousand years ago, everything changed. We have been given rest. This is our newness of life in Christ! Every oppressor—sin, death, sickness, disease, poverty—has been stilled. Their onslaught is over! Yahweh shattered the authority of these wicked rulers!

The entire world is at rest and bursts forth with singing. All mankind is free to enjoy the benefits of abundant life. We are a beautiful new creation, co-resurrected with Christ, seated with Him in heavenly places.

"Talking about our co-seatedness, I want you to see something! Oh wow! What I see takes my breath away! A wide-open door in the heavenly realm! The first thing I heard was this voice addressing me! It was distinct and clear, like the sound of a trumpet; it captured my attention, inviting me to enter. "Come up here and I will show you how everything coincides with what you have already seen!" So here I am, immersed in this unrestricted space of spirit ecstasy. As the vision opens, I immediately notice the throne and One seated upon it."

— Revelation 4:1-2 (Mirror Bible)

"I saw a portal open into the heavenly realm, and the same trumpet-voice I heard speaking with me at the beginning said, "Ascend into this realm! I want to reveal to you what must happen after this." ² *Instantly I was taken into the spirit realm and behold—I saw a heavenly throne being set in place and someone seated upon it."*
— Revelation 4:1-2 (Passion Translation)

This is not speaking of a future day. This is now! The trumpet is the Awakening Blast calling us into this open portal to ascend into the wide-open door of the heavenly realm. John did not simply look through the door and see these things happen as something afar off, as a future event someday. He was transported through the open door into the heavenly realm. He said in verse 2, "Instantly I was taken in the spirit realm." Literally, that means I came to be within Spirit.

John was overwhelmed or engulfed in the Spirit... in the Presence behind the veil, seeing with His eyes all that awaited him.

We have been invited to live life in the limitless possibilities, the thrilling adventure that lies before us in this beautiful place called IT IS FINISHED now here on earth. This is our reality. This is our inheritance. This is the victorious life we are called to live.

Are you ready to step into this reality? Are you ready to embrace the fullness of what Christ has accomplished? The door is wide open. The invitation is clear. Step into the limitless, the boundless, the finished work of Christ. Live in the ecstatic joy and overwhelming peace of being co-seated with Him.

IT IS FINISHED!

Are you ready to step boldly into your new life?

About the Author

DR. ROBIN SMIT is a gifted author and teacher committed to the message of the Finished Work of Jesus Christ. She has a ThD and an MA in Theology and Biblical Studies. Dr. Smit is a well-respected voice in the message of grace, highlighted by a wide array of contributions. She is the founder of TWS Publishing and a co-founding partner of GAN TV.

Her teachings have inspired and empowered countless readers, helping them deepen their understanding of God's grace and its life-changing impact on their spiritual journey.

She and her husband reside in California and Tennessee.

Also by by Robin Smit

It Is Finished

Awakened

I am Healed

Free to Give (CO-AUTHORED WITH 11 OTHER AUTHORS)

Behold the Lamb